T0279746

Thoughtful Aging

Restoring Honor to the Aging Process

Alina Wilson

Thoughtful Aging LLC
18840 SW Boones Ferry Road, Suite 140
Tualatin, OR 97062
ThoughtfulAgingBook.com

ISBN: 979-8-9903809-1-2 (paperback)
ISBN: 979-8-9903809-0-5 (hardcover)
ISBN: 979-8-9903809-2-9 (ebook)
ISBN: 979-8-9903809-3-6 (audiobook)

To my parents, whose spiritual guidance, belief that anything is possible, and lifetime pursuit of truth have left their fingerprints throughout these pages. I carry these traits with honor.

To my children, who choose to see beyond the surface of my humanity: Your wisdom and reflection are why this book exists.

And to my grandchildren, Carley, Kathryn, and Sawyer, yours is the generation of realignment to true beauty. Be the leaders, not the followers.

Foreword

When was the last time you looked in the mirror and truly saw yourself? Not just the lines and wrinkles that mark the passage of time, but the woman who has lived, loved, and learned through every one of those years? In a world that often tells us to focus on our imperfections, it takes a special kind of courage to see past those surface-level details and recognize the beauty, wisdom, and strength that come with age. This is what Alina Wilson does so beautifully in *Thoughtful Aging: Restoring Honor to the Aging Process*.

Alina's work is more than just a book; it's a call to arms for women everywhere to reclaim their power and redefine what it means to age. With the precision of a scientist and the empathy of a sister, she dismantles the toxic narratives that the anti-aging industry has spun around us for far too long. She reminds us that aging is not something to be feared or fought against, but something to be embraced with grace and confidence.

I've always believed in the power of storytelling to heal, to inspire, and to change the world. Alina's story, woven throughout the pages of this book, does exactly that. She not only shares her deep understanding of the beauty industry, but also exposes the ways in which it has systematically eroded our self-esteem. She lays bare the harsh truths about how big business has capitalized on our insecurities, selling us the idea that our worth is tied to our youthfulness. But Alina doesn't leave us in the darkness of these revelations; instead, she lights a path forward, guiding us toward a new understanding of beauty, that is rooted in self-acceptance and empowerment.

Reading *Thoughtful Aging*, I couldn't help but think of the women who have come before me—my mother, my grandmothers, and my great-grandmothers—who navigated their own battles with society's narrow definition of beauty, much as we do today. I started modeling as a child in the '80s, which was predictable given that my mother was a model and my father was an art director. My early years and life experiences molded my sense of worth around how I looked on the outside. I was a very tall girl, and being a size 2 was never going to happen, which led to an eating disorder in my teens.

It wasn't until I had my own daughter in the 2000s that I started to notice how I was projecting those same societal pressures onto her. I saw how distorted my view of my body had become, shaped by years of trying to fit into an impossible ideal. This realization was a turning point for me, but it is still something I struggle with every day. As I approach the big five-0, Alina's message in *Thoughtful Aging* resonates deeply with me because it challenges the narrative that has dominated my life for far too long. It has opened my eyes to the need for a healthier, more compassionate way to view ourselves as we age. It's a reminder for all of us that our worth is not tied to our youth or our size, and that true beauty comes from the richness of our experiences, the depth of our wisdom, and the authenticity with which we live our lives.

Alina's message is clear: It's time to take back our power by reclaiming our self-worth and redefining what it means to be beautiful. It's about breaking free from the chains of societal expectations and stepping into a new era of self-love and acceptance. And it couldn't come at a more crucial time. As we face an increasingly image-driven world, where social media and advertising constantly bombard us with unrealistic standards, *Thoughtful Aging* offers a much-needed counter-narrative—one that empowers us to see ourselves in a new light.

So, as you turn the pages of this book, I encourage you to take Alina's words to heart. Let them inspire you to look in the mirror and see not just the woman you were or the woman you wish you could be, but the woman you are right now—beautiful, strong, and worthy of every good thing life has to offer. Aging is not the enemy; it's a journey, and with Alina as your guide, it's one you can embrace with open arms.

Thank you, Alina, for giving us this powerful, transformative book. It's a gift to women everywhere, and I am honored to be a part of this journey with you.

With gratitude,

Anna-Mieke Anderson

Founder and active CEO of MiaDonna & Company and nonprofit The Greener Diamond

CONTENTS

Introduction

If you're looking for a book that will offer you a pathway to wisdom, confidence, and a deeper understanding of your unique beauty, you've found it.

This is not a guide to effortless perfection, nor a manual filled with quick fixes and empty promises. Instead, it's an invitation to embrace yourself as you are, flaws and all, and find power in your journey toward radical self-acceptance. I won't claim to have all the answers, but I can promise you this: Through the challenges I have faced, I have gained insights that I am deeply honored to share with you. Together, we'll explore what it means to age with dignity, grace, and a renewed sense of self-worth.

I opened my first medical aesthetics clinic in 2007. Since then, I have spoken to thousands of women about their experiences with aging. I have watched them navigate the complexities of change, and I have experienced my own journey. I have seen firsthand how many women feel compelled to fight aging, believing their worth is tied to a youthful appearance. But I have also seen women embrace their age, radiate beauty from within, and defy the societal messages that try to limit them.

I wrote this book because I believe that every woman is beautiful, and to invite women like you to see and feel it, even if just for a moment. My goal is to help you see through society's deceptive messaging that says you are not enough. I believe that every woman deserves to look in the mirror and love who she sees, just as she is.

Aging isn't something to resist or fear; it's an opportunity to grow, to honor who we've become, and to find beauty in the imperfections that make us human. I invite you to join me as we explore how to let go of impossible standards and cherish the uniqueness that defines us instead. By the end of this book, I am confident that you will see yourself—and your life's journey—in a new, more compassionate light.

We will dive deep into how the anti-aging industry has shaped our perceptions and, more importantly, how to let go of external expectations and reclaim our narratives. This book will guide you through practical steps to align with your own Thoughtful Aging process, touching on the power of mindset, the influence of relationships, and what it means to reconnect with the deep inner wisdom our bodies hold. Together, we will discover that the true essence of beauty lies within, waiting to be fully realized and celebrated.

As we go through this journey, my hope is that you not only see yourself more clearly, but also experience a newfound confidence that radiates from the inside out. This transformation will change the way you move through the world. You are already beautiful, and this book invites you to believe it fully, without hesitation.

Your story is not over—it's just beginning. Let's redefine aging with honor, grace, and a celebration of the life that's still unfolding.

Chapter 1:

What No One Tells You About Anti-Aging

We have created a culture that tells women the most important thing they can be is beautiful. Then we pummel them with a standard of beauty they will never meet. After that, when they worry about beauty, we call them superficial.

—From *Beauty Sick: How the Cultural Obsession with Appearance Hurts Girls and Women*[1]

One of the gifts of wisdom is knowing when to stop. Wise women know when to stop chasing the illusion of perfection and when to stop clinging to the past. They know when to stop resisting the inevitable changes that come with time.

Within months of opening my first medical aesthetics clinic back in 2007, I saw a pattern emerge in my conversations with patients. These beautiful women, from all walks of life, kept sharing the same negative comments about their appearance. They would arrive at the clinic hopeful, seeking the latest and greatest treatments to "fix" what they saw as flaws. Those flaws might be bags under their eyes, dark spots on their skin, the size of their lips or cheeks or, of course, their wrinkles. As I listened to their concerns, I noticed something else: These women were no longer seeing their own beauty. Instead, they were fixated on what they perceived as imperfections.

This troubled me, in part because I recognized the pattern in myself. How could it be that women from such diverse backgrounds shared the same anxieties about their appearance? Where did these deeply ingrained ideas come from? Each conversation centered around one theme: "anti-aging." It became clear to me that these women had come to believe that a reversal of aging is not only desirable, but also attainable. This belief, and their fixation on it, was distracting them from their true beauty.

MY EXPERIENCE OF FEELING INVISIBLE

My life's work has been to help women see their beauty. I wrote this book because I want to help women break free from the false beliefs around aging and anti-aging culture so they can see their true beauty. We will cover this in detail throughout the book, but to start, I want to share with you my own experience of living a life based on chasing ideals rather than authenticity.

From an early age, I began checking off all the boxes society told me would lead to a fulfilling life. I married a man for what I thought was love, started a family, and ran a successful in-home daycare business, looking after as many as fourteen children each day so that I could be the perfect stay-at-home mother. I felt as if the life I was living was the life I was choosing. Yet as time went on, I began to feel a disconnection growing within. By the time I approached my mid-thirties, I had developed a strange sense that I was becoming a ghost in my own life, a shadow of the vibrant woman I had always imagined myself to be.

This feeling wasn't tied to any particular aspect of my life; it wasn't just about my children or my career choices. I was happy that my children were becoming independent and living their own lives as they entered their late teens, but it also left me wondering where I fit in. While I was proud of them, I missed the days when they turned to me for guidance and comfort. My interactions with them now felt more like polite exchanges, which left me wondering if I was doing something wrong.

I also noticed a shift after opening the aesthetics clinic. By that time, I had married again, and my physician husband dreamed of working independently, outside of a broken healthcare system. I worked hard to make that dream a reality, but all too soon, I found myself feeling out of place amongst all the beautiful women who passed through our doors each day. I began to question why I could see their beauty but not my own.

In my marriage, a distance had grown between me and my husband. Our relationship had settled into a predictable routine, one built around the formality of running a business together. It lacked the compassion and connection we once shared. I knew he felt it, too, but despite all our efforts, we had simply accepted this quiet coexistence as the new normal.

I noticed that people's reactions to me had changed when I was out in public, too; I seemed to blend into the background and no longer elicited the same warmth or responsiveness from strangers, service staff, or even acquaintances at social gatherings. I felt a pervasive, creeping sense of becoming less visible, less relevant, and found myself wondering if it was them or me. I didn't crave excessive attention or need to be noticed, but I did want to feel seen and valued, to know that my presence still mattered. I couldn't quite pinpoint when I had started to feel this way or exactly how to express it. It was as if the world was moving forward while I was being left behind.

Then there was my appearance. In years past, I had avoided mirrors, but now I was being called back to them. When I looked in the mirror, I saw someone who looked tired. With each year that went by, I had more wrinkles. My skin sagged a bit. I had put on weight that I just couldn't seem to get rid of. Had I let myself go? Not really, but my appearance *had* changed. I began to wonder if my feeling of invisibility and my cooled relationship were connected to this change as well.

I had always taken care of myself, but now, all I could see were signs of aging. The lines in my face, the deep creases between my brows, the gray constantly reappearing in my hair, and the weight around my middle bothered me more and more. By this time, the clinic had been open for a year and a half. I had yet to try Botox or any other treatments. I, like many women to whom I have spoken, wasn't sure I wanted to change my appearance or become dependent on products to feel good about myself. After all, wasn't it virtuous to "age gracefully"? But I didn't feel good about myself. I thought if I could just improve one thing that really bothered me, I might be able to regain a feeling of relevance.

Within three months of my first Botox treatment, the deep lines between my brows softened. Within three months of my second treatment, they were completely gone. Changing one thing wasn't enough, though. I started to notice the way my left cheek drooped more than my right, affecting my smile. This was a result of an untreated Bell's palsy condition I had experienced as a young adult. So, I furthered my exploration into the world of aesthetics and used dermal filler to restore symmetry to my face.

I then began to ask women who seemed to defy time what their secrets were. I spent hours researching and learning about skin care products, what active ingredients could truly improve skin health, and how combining laser treatments with at-home products offered hope for those seeking a more natural aging process. Without realizing it, I had become consumed by an industry offering eternal youth. The results from each new product or treatment brought me a fleeting sense of hope, but those results were never quite enough.

What I didn't realize was that the belief driving my pursuit of anti-aging was fundamentally flawed. I hadn't lost my place in the world because of my appearance; I had lost it because I had internalized a cultural narrative that told me I was only desirable if I looked young. The real issue wasn't the lines on my face but the belief that those lines made me less significant, less worthy of attention.

I'll share more of my story later in the book. For now, let's explore *why* I turned to anti-aging treatments rather than embracing the changes and growth that come with aging.

WHY ANTI-AGING DOESN'T WORK

The negativity and denial of anti-aging is inherent in the word itself. Right there, in the first half of the word: "anti." Anti-aging—as an industry and as an idea—calls on us to fight against ourselves. How many ads or product descriptions have you read that promise to "combat" the signs of aging?

The "battle" against aging, fueled by the very word "anti," traps us in a mindset of resistance. We are encouraged to "combat" the signs of aging, as if aging itself is an enemy to be defeated. But in this light, we end up battling our own natural processes, rejecting parts of ourselves in pursuit of a fleeting ideal. This negativity and denial can distance us from the true essence of who we are, leaving us chasing an unattainable version of youth instead of embracing the richness of life's later stages.

As an approach to aging, anti-aging doesn't do us any favors. It doesn't work, to begin with. But it also sees only the downsides of aging and none of its many benefits. Of course, if you want to sell an anti-aging product or an anti-aging mindset, you don't talk about the upsides of aging. You might even pretend they don't exist.

Anti-aging diminishes us in another way, too: it attempts to erase our experience. It promotes the idea that the signs of aging, such as wrinkles and gray hair, are flaws to be corrected rather than markers of a life well lived. The messages in anti-aging product marketing, or even in conversations with our friends, suggest that we should conceal our aging. There is an underlying assumption that aging is bad, even something to be feared. But concealing these aspects of ourselves also undermines the value of the experience, wisdom, and personal growth that account for so much of who we are.

There is power in our life experience. Dishonoring this experience by being insecure about how our looks change as we age does a disservice to ourselves and everyone else. Too often, we view our wrinkles as flaws. But what they represent is a lifetime of experience and the character that develops.

Anti-aging has deceived us in another way: it demands we look backward rather than forward. It literally sells the idea of "turning back time." Powerful women—wise women—know to look forward while staying grounded in the present moment. Too often, the pursuit of anti-aging is, at least in part, an attempt to hold on to the past.

Finally, an anti-aging approach also distracts us from the emotional work we need to do. It stunts our growth. The pursuit of youth is often a distraction from the deeper work of self-acceptance.

So... how do you feel about all this? Are you ready to put this book down and walk away? Or are you bracing yourself for a lecture about how focusing on our appearance is vain or shallow? There will be no lectures from me. I'm not saying we *have* to live with wrinkles and other signs of aging. We choose how to manage our appearance and what looking our best means to us. But we can't see ourselves or our wrinkles clearly until we can see past what anti-aging culture has taught us.

Given all the downsides of the anti-aging approach, the question really is: Why have we fallen for all of the false narratives about aging? I believe it is because we have become disconnected from our true beauty. This is easy to do in the age of distraction. There is a great deal of noise in our culture, and society's messaging about anti-aging and how women should look is especially loud. But it is wrong. How women actually experience aging is *very* different from what the media and society tell us. The research I did for this book and other third-party studies confirm this. Women's actual experience of aging is significantly better than the anti-aging industry would have us believe.

But let's stay with our inquiry into anti-aging culture. Let's look at what the media and society have to say about women, their appearance, and aging.

THE TRAIT SOCIETY
VALUES MOST IN WOMEN

According to a Pew Research Center survey of 4,500 people, the trait society values most in women is "physical attractiveness."[2] Note that this survey expressly uses the word "value"—physical attractiveness is what society *values* most in women. It follows, then, that as our attractiveness—however that is defined—wanes, our value in society wanes.

So, *does* our value in society wane as we get older? Many women think so. Part of my research for this book was to survey 1,000 women about their experiences and opinions around aging, beauty, and appearance. One of the questions I asked them was: "What do you think of this statement? A woman's value in society diminishes as she ages." More than 40% of the women said they do feel a woman's value diminishes as she ages.

THE #1 BEAUTY STANDARD

For me, the next question was: "Does a woman's attractiveness wane as she gets older—or, at least, does society tell us this?" Then there was the obvious follow-up question: "Does youthfulness equate to beauty?"

Anti-aging culture answered that immediately: Yes. Messaging that youthfulness equates to beauty is everywhere, constantly. And there are many studies that back up that perception. "Reducing signs of aging" is the most popular beauty standard among women of all age groups, from eighteen-year-olds to women over sixty, according to an AARP survey of 7,000 women. And the second most-mentioned beauty standard? "Using Botox and fillers."[3] Which is, of course, directly related to anti-aging as well.

Let's pause here for a moment. I want to be clear: There's nothing right or wrong with using products like neurotoxins or facial fillers to enhance your appearance. Ideas of "right" or "wrong" come from judgment, and judgment has no place in the conversation when it comes to personal expression. Imagine how liberating it would be to live without judgment, whether we are imposing judgment on someone or having someone else impose their judgment on us!

The discussion here is not about judging personal decisions. What we are talking about is the harmful pursuit of anti-aging as an attainable goal. If you find yourself having judgmental thoughts as you read this book, I invite you to pause and examine their source.

My own research, and that by others, suggests that conventional attractiveness and youthfulness are closely linked and that women's value in society diminishes as they age *because they no longer look youthful, i.e., as attractive.* For most women, this is no surprise. But I wanted to see how much of an impact this was having on women's experiences of aging.

I asked the women I surveyed: "What is the biggest problem with aging as a woman in American culture?" The most-mentioned problem was becoming invisible or losing value in society. Some women paired the two feelings (becoming invisible and losing value) as part of the same experience.

Here is how some of the women responded:

- *You become invisible as you get older. Many are used to attention when young, and once you get past a certain age, no one looks at you anymore.*

- *We are invisible as soon as we aren't gorgeous.*

- *Women at a certain age are almost completely ignored by society, as if we have nothing to say or contribute once we reach a certain age.*

- *As we age, we become invisible.*

- *I feel that women are dismissed and ignored when they begin to look a certain age.*

- *The problem is that women at a certain age become invisible. Women are always being held to unrealistic physical standards. I enjoy my age and maturity and wish women could age without feeling pressure to be something they are not.*

There were pages more of comments like these. All of them echoed the same sentiment. Some women expressed genuine pain from being sidelined. The experience of feeling invisible is not true for all women, but it is familiar to most of us. It affects some women's mental health. Add the challenges of perimenopause and menopause, the possibility of being sidelined or laid off because of ageism at work, and the all-too-common phenomenon of being "replaced" by a younger woman in one's marriage or partnership, and it is wholly reasonable for women to be concerned about how they look. It is understandable that so many women want to look younger. We are not being shallow or vain. We are being practical. The consequences of not looking young are real.

The noise of societal expectations, the pressures of appearance, the weight of comparison—these all conspire to make even the strongest of women feel invisible. And yet, there is power in naming and acknowledging the struggle. By exploring the true source of this influence, we can reemerge and reclaim our sense of worth despite the noise.

THE BEAUTY INDUSTRY IS NOT THE SOURCE OF THE PROBLEM

We typically blame the media, advertising, or the beauty industry for the pressure women feel to look attractive. But it is actually society, more than the beauty industry, that has shaped the false narrative of aging. One of the most surprising results of my research was that only two out of the 1,000 women I surveyed said the beauty industry is the real problem or underlying issue with aging as a woman in America. But almost every single woman who took the survey mentioned the influence of society at some point. Did you catch that? The beauty industry takes a back seat to society.

This is not conventional wisdom. But rather than immediately pin all the responsibility for anti-aging thinking on the beauty industry (though they are hardly innocent), let's focus on the true source of the problem: society.

Messaging from society creates the foundation for anti-aging pressures by promoting the idea that youth is more valuable than age. The beauty industry capitalizes on these societal values, but it is society's underlying message that makes us susceptible to the industry's promises. Ultimately, we internalize these societal beliefs and act on them, driving the demand for anti-aging products. Yes, the ads, the products, and the descriptions influence us. Yes, anti-aging messaging is everywhere. But the industry and its advertising are only playing on our existing desires and insecurities. These desires and insecurities are driven by society. The messaging from society influences us so powerfully because we believe it. We respond to the messaging and the ads from the beauty industry because of the beliefs our society has imbued in us.

I remember subtle comments and messages I absorbed growing up, like my mother and her sisters worrying about looking old in photos, magazine covers celebrating youthful celebrities, and friends swapping tips for staying young and thin. It was everywhere. Society taught me—and others, of course—that my aging wasn't just inevitable, it was something to fight. As I noticed my daughter mimicking the same behaviors, I realized that the pressure I felt didn't come from the latest anti-wrinkle cream I had purchased or a Maybelline commercial. It was woven into the world around me, into everyday conversations and expectations. The beauty industry was just expanding on a story society had already written.

It's time to start questioning why we buy into the narrative at all. It isn't the industry that made us feel this way. It's society. And maybe, just maybe, it's time to stop believing the lie.

"SOCIETY" IS US

So it's not the beauty industry that's primarily shaping the false narrative about aging. It's "society." That seems like an easy explanation until you start to really think about it. Who is "society," exactly? *It's us.* According to extensive research from AARP, when it comes to beauty and appearance, women are more influenced by other women than anything else: Women under fifty cite friends or their "social circle" as their number one source of influence for beauty and appearance. Their second most common source of influence is "what they see from women around them"—so again, other women.

Even social media, which is incredibly influential, is a secondary influence compared to women's friends and what they see and hear from other women. And advertising? That's the third most powerful source of influence on women's beliefs about beauty and appearance.

If you're wondering where men fit into all this, that same study shows that men are the *least* influential source for women's ideas about beauty and appearance.[4]

Here's the key takeaway: If women are the source of the most influence on women, then we have an opportunity for change. The way we wield our influence and approach our own aging can create an opportunity for ourselves and for other women. We can reframe the discussion around aging. We can reimagine what aging means. But first, let's talk about social media.

HOW SOCIAL MEDIA AFFECTS WOMEN

Social media has evolved to show us an endless stream of perfectly curated images of women—many middle-aged or older—who seem to have defied time entirely. Their faces are smooth, their bodies toned, and their lives appear effortlessly glamorous, usually thanks to careful curation and image filters.

How do you feel when you see these presentations? How much of your own struggle has been influenced by these carefully crafted portrayals of beauty and youth? The influence of social media cannot be overstated, especially for younger women.

According to AARP's research, about half of all women admit social media has some influence on their beauty choices. Women between the ages of eighteen and forty-nine are more likely to be influenced by Instagram than other platforms. For women fifty and over, Facebook has the most impact.[5]

It was strange to me that only half of the women in the AARP survey said social media influenced their beauty choices. But when I asked the women in my survey how social media has affected how they feel about aging, 38.6% said social media didn't affect them, either.

Of course, we often are unaware that we are being influenced. Influence can come through a single memorable event, but much of it is just due to repetition over time invisibly shaping our views. And there are plenty of women who never or rarely use social media. No matter what role it plays in your life, it is important to be mindful of how it affects you.

For most of us, it does have an effect: Approximately 40% of the women I surveyed said social media has a negative impact on them, while more than 10% said it has a *significant* negative impact on them.

> I think it is okay to show your age, but America makes you feel like you're giving up your femininity if you're not covering up evidence of your age, which creates sadness and depression. And yet I cannot help but feel that same pressure as well.
>
> —Survey respondent

HOW ANTI-AGING CULTURE HARMS US

The idea of anti-aging is so omnipresent in our lives that we may not have any context for an alternate approach. After all, messaging about how important it is to look youthful is so prevalent and persuasive that "girls as young as 8 are turning up at dermatologists' offices with rashes, chemical burns and other allergic reactions to products not intended for children's sensitive skin."[6] Early in 2024, the state of California attempted to pass legislation that would block thirteen-year-olds from buying certain anti-aging products because those products can damage their skin so badly.

Anti-aging messaging is clearly harming our daughters and granddaughters, but it's also harming us. Even if we have a grounded sense of self and are not caught up in trying to look younger at any cost, we are not isolated from the world around us. The idea that you are "less valuable" because of your age did not originate with you, and you are not shallow or superficial for wanting to look younger. Anti-aging messaging is so widespread and often so well disguised; we don't even recognize it after a while. We just very slowly accept it, then internalize it, then turn it upon ourselves.

Women are easy targets for anti-aging messaging because of a number of unexamined beliefs. These beliefs drive anti-aging as an idea and as an industry.

These ideas are further amplified by media outlets that increasingly determine what we see and how we understand what we see. If all we see are advertisements and television shows with perfect-looking, youthful women, we come to expect that everyone should look like that. Then technology shapes our views even further through social media filters, photoshopping, and the algorithms that amplify viral—and usually anti-aging—messaging. This distorts how we view and even experience the aging process.

I have seen this cycle for myself many times, but one consultation appointment a few years ago was especially troubling. A young woman in her mid-twenties had scheduled the appointment to talk about her skin health. Upon entering the treatment room, she proceeded to pull out her phone and open her Snapchat app, showing a filtered photo of herself. She stated that she wanted whatever treatments would make her "look like the photo." We explained to her that we could not make her look like a Snapchat filter. She didn't seem to hear or understand. We explained that it was a filter, not real, and therefore that result was unattainable. We shared with her what could be done, and she again asked if the suggested treatments would make her "look like the photo." After a few more attempts to explain to her that we simply cannot make someone look like a Snapchat-filtered photo, she left disappointed and did not return. Social media had literally altered her sense of reality.

To help all of us get free from these potent, warping influences, let's take a hard look at the ideas underpinning anti-aging. Once we can see some of the broken assumptions that fuel this mindset, we can stop getting caught up in it.

The anti-aging industry and culture are founded on these false beliefs:

- Youthfulness equates to beauty
- A woman's most valuable asset is her looks
- To be beautiful, you must look a certain way
- Aging is inherently bad, a de facto period of decline
- We can stop aging

Let's unpack each of these misconceptions.

YOUTHFULNESS EQUATES TO BEAUTY

Everywhere, overt and covert messages convey that as we age, we become less beautiful. And yet despite all those messages, most women say they believe in and support the "beauty of aging"—at least for other women. Of female consumers polled in a 2023 study, 82% said that a woman should be proud to look her true age, though 67% of these women still admitted to being self-conscious about their looks as they grow older.[7] I wonder how many of those 67% were self-conscious about their looks when they were younger, too. Probably most of them.

I want to reassert here that there is no "right" or "wrong" about wanting to look our best. What matters more is valuing ourselves and our experience. If we are connected to our intuition and our wisdom, and know our value and our beauty, we don't need to look younger to feel beautiful. We already are beautiful. If that is the foundation of our experience, we can seek to enhance or adjust our appearance however we please, and it will be just that—an enhancement, not a necessity.

> **The secret to beauty is really embracing who you are and loving your body, face, and hair color as they change naturally, instead of giving your money to doctors and aestheticians and believing the lie that you must stay as young-looking as possible.**
>
> **—Survey respondent**

In all fairness, the anti-aging industry has made some steps toward acknowledging the beauty of older women, though it still portrays beauty as youthfulness most of the time. But perhaps the industry is actually a bit behind the times.

In a recent study that asked 2,000 Americans about their beliefs around aging and beauty, 73% of the respondents agreed with the statement, "Beauty is ageless." Curiously, the younger they were, the more likely they were to agree:

84% of Gen Zers (born after 1996) agreed with the statement

73% of Millennials (born 1981–1996) agreed

72% of Gen Xers (born 1965–1980) agreed

67% of Boomers (born 1946–1964) agreed

Women were especially likely to agree that beauty is ageless: 81% of the women in this survey did, compared to 65% of the men. But—just as in the study I cited at the opening of this section—when it came to their own aging, the women in this survey were not quite as pro-aging. Only 57% of them said they were comfortable with their own aging, versus 70% of men.[8]

A WOMAN'S MOST VALUABLE ASSET IS HER LOOKS

Pew surveys aside, this is obviously untrue. For a woman's most valuable asset to be her looks, appearances would have to supersede all other things. They don't.

Who would you rather be, a brilliant businesswoman with the skills and tenacity to build an empire or an unusually pretty girl? Which of those two people has the better "asset"? What would you rather have: unflinching confidence or the cheekbones, skin, right-shaped eyes, and mouth to qualify as beautiful? Almost all women would rather have the confidence. That is the "asset" that can get you anything beauty can, plus a whole lot more.

One survey respondent told us: "I was verrrry [sic] attractive when I was younger. I never thought my looks were the best thing about me. Still don't."

ARE WOMEN COMPLICIT?

When we try to make ourselves look younger, do we acquiesce to anti-aging culture, at least to a degree? Perhaps, and that is not a comfortable thing to realize. It is very much like how, when you make yourself more attractive, you play into that cultural dynamic; in a way, you reinforce society's tendency to evaluate people based on their looks. And yet, if you take the purist's route and, say, go without makeup and eschew fashion or even basic grooming, you are likely to experience some sidelining.

So, what should we do? We need to navigate society, so we must at least address certain expectations about our appearance. We have every right to take care of ourselves and be proud of how we look. And yet, we risk reinforcing stereotypes by shifting our appearance to look more youthful.

There is no perfect resolution to this quandary. Each woman will have to decide for herself what she is comfortable with and be aware of how her comfort levels may shift over the years or even in different situations.

TO BE BEAUTIFUL, YOU MUST LOOK A CERTAIN WAY

We constantly compare ourselves to others based on standards created by society, which are then exploited by the beauty industry and social media channels. This is not just an apples-to-apples comparison, either. We compare our real-world looks to the photoshopped, filtered, professionally photographed, professionally made up, and professionally lit faces and bodies of people who are in the top 0.1% of attractiveness. No wonder we feel insecure.

This comparison game starts early, too: Girls as young as four are aware of being "too fat."[9] Many young women in their early twenties get Botox, lip filler, or other procedures, often simply because a friend of theirs got a similar procedure. All of this gets showcased on social media, further amplifying the trend.

Reality TV shows like *The Kardashians* and *Love Island* are also a major influence on young people and regularly show women who might qualify as having overdone their treatments. Contestants and celebrities in these shows have foreheads that don't move, oversized lips, massive eyelashes, and often Brazilian butt lifts (BBLs). Depending on which generation you belong to, these altered features can seem beautiful or quite unattractive. The fallacy lies in thinking that it has to be all or nothing. Yes, some women choose to enhance their features, but that's not the only option. Other women choose a more natural look. For example, treatments with Botox can be done in a way that allows the patient to retain some movement in their forehead but also relaxes the muscles enough that they don't form deep, permanent lines and wrinkles. Based on what we're shown in anti-aging commerce and on some television shows, you wouldn't know this option exists.

AGING IS INHERENTLY BAD,
A DE FACTO PERIOD OF DECLINE

Aging may be a period of decline for some women, but not for all. There are just as many studies and statistics that show women's lives actually improve as they age.

Women "truly come into their own authentic self at age 42, on average"

According to AARP's researchers, forty-two is the age when women are most likely to feel like they are truly themselves.[10] To be truly, authentically oneself is a profound gift. To achieve that is not a sign of a life in decline.

Forty-two is an interesting age to pick because it also happens to be three years after women typically begin to feel pressure to look younger. Could "causality" be at play here, or is it just coincidence? After a few years of feeling pressure to look younger, do some or even most women begin to ignore the anti-aging messaging from society and the media? I hope so.

The "U of happiness"

The "U of happiness" refers to a finding in the 2024 World Happiness Report that people's happiness typically declines in their twenties, thirties, and forties, and then begins to improve significantly in their fifties. The happiest people in the world, according to this globally recognized study, are American women over sixty.[11] Again, this is not a sign of a group whose lives are in decline.

Women tend to feel more comfortable with themselves as they age

According to an AARP study, 76% of women over fifty agree with the statement, "I feel more comfortable in my own skin." That's higher than the 68% of women aged eighteen to forty-nine who agree. Women over fifty are also more likely to say, "I am kinder to myself about my body image as I age," "I celebrate my body as I age," "I feel free to dress how I want," and "I do not have a negative body image." Women over fifty are also less likely to feel pressure to meet beauty standards.[12]

So again, women's actual experience with aging is very different than what anti-aging commerce and societal messages tell us it is. These three studies show that.

Many women become happier as they age. We find beauty in ourselves much more easily than we did before. This has been expressed to me many times over by older women at the clinic. It showed up in my research as well. This AARP study found that "Women 50-plus (75%) are more likely than those ages 18 to 49 (65%) to measure their beauty based on their own sense of self rather than needing to compare themselves to others... In fact, the vast majority (95%) see an overall sense of well-being as more important than outer beauty."[13]

IS LIFE BETTER AFTER FIFTY?

Given all the evidence of women's lives improving as they age, could it be that life after fifty is actually better than life before it? I asked women what the best thing about being over fifty is. The most frequent answer was that you stop caring about what people think. The second most common answer was "wisdom," as in the wisdom that comes with maturity. Third place was a tie between having more confidence, being true to yourself, and having less stress. And that sounds very good to me.

BEYOND ANTI-AGING

This is what I want you to take away from this chapter: Aging can be a good thing. Aging can be something that happens *for* us rather than *to* us. We have the power to see the world and ourselves however we like. We can decide what is beautiful or not. We are the ones who get to choose what beauty is for us.

Instead of trying to look twenty or thirty again, we can look forward to our happiest years. We can reframe the negative attitudes toward aging that have made it unnecessarily hard and caused so much pain to so many women. Our daughters and granddaughters, nieces and neighbors, colleagues, and younger friends all need to know that aging is vastly different from and better than the story they've been sold.

To restore honor to the aging process, we must find a more fulfilling and meaningful approach to aging. With a more thoughtful approach to aging, we can learn to embrace the changes that come with aging rather than try to fight them.

Chapter 2:

Thoughtful Aging: A Different Approach

What if you could look in the mirror and have your first thought be, "I am beautiful"? If you've not had that experience before, I promise you: it is possible.

The Greek root of the word "beauty" is related to the word for "calling," to "kalon" and "kalein."[14] Beauty is actually calling us: calling us back to ourselves, to be ourselves, to pursue growth, and to integrate our knowledge into wisdom. It's as if we hear an inner voice saying, *Return inward. Your strength is here. This is where you are meant to be.* Until we answer that call, we will always carry a yearning, a longing, a sense of vacancy.

You can *feel* beautiful even when you do not think you *look* "beautiful," or at least look beautiful according to American beauty standards. It is possible to learn to look past those beauty standards to see your very own singular beauty—the spark you alone embody, your very best features, your uniqueness. You can love who you see in the mirror no matter your age.

You have the power to change how you see yourself. You do not need money, treatments, makeup, filters, or products to do this; it is entirely up to you. It is you seeing yourself, your beautiful self, just as you are. Even if you do not believe this right now, I urge you to stay with me. Keep reading.

I can show you how to see that beautiful you because I have been through this process myself. As a teen and young adult, I constantly criticized my body. At age fourteen, I was a size 8, but I felt I was overweight. I had heard the term "muffin top" and became fixated on that as a problem. At size 8, I didn't really have extra body fat hanging over my jeans unless I wore that one low-rise pair. That was enough to make it true.

This was a turning point for me, and not a good one. I began to subconsciously view my body as the enemy. It was no longer the body with which I had flowed through each day in harmony; it was now fighting against me. As my view of my body shifted, I began to see even more problems: dry, frizzy hair, large pores on my face, and rough skin, to name a few. Somewhere along the way, I heard the term "thunder thighs" and adopted that, too. Looking for my physical deficiencies became part of my daily routine. My body had not changed; my *perception* of my body had changed.

Once I allowed that narrative to take root in my mind, it became my new reality. My mind and my body were no longer in partnership. I faulted my body for the natural changes of adolescence. Then I went from a size 8 to a size 12 within a couple of years. This new reality affected how I expressed myself in group settings, and my confidence in speaking up and using my voice. I became quietly insecure about my worth and questioned whether I could ever be loved with all these imperfections. This led to what became an unhealthy pattern of attention-seeking behavior.

I've spoken with countless women who have shared similar stories with me. Somehow, we arrived at a place of disconnection, not quite sure how we got there, and fighting negative thoughts about how we looked. But our stories don't have to end there. There is a way to embrace new ideas and practices that will help us look in the mirror and think: "I feel beautiful. And I *am* beautiful."

The most obvious, immediate way to have that experience is to simply change your appearance. As women, we do this all the time by choosing a new hairstyle, a new lipstick, or a new outfit. I did this myself. I created a rigorous program and sought out the best resources to address my imperfections. Remember the ThighMaster? Suzanne Somers had me convinced it would solve all my problems. It, too, became another reminder of the disappointment I felt in my inability to achieve perfection.

Changing how we look works for a while, but if we don't look to our inner beauty as much as we look to our outer beauty, we always seem to end up in the same place... seeking more change. Somehow, or at some point, swapping out makeup and changing our hair, our clothes, or our skin care regimen doesn't achieve what we really want.

I'll talk about several ways to reconnect with your beauty in this book, but to start, I'd like to explore the practice of radical self-acceptance so you can see and love yourself as you truly are. Ultimately, self-acceptance is the only way to fully embrace your beauty and how you choose to present yourself in the world.

Fully embracing your beauty is about more than just enhancing your appearance, though that may also happen along the way. When your mind and body are connected, there are no limits to what you can do or who you can be. No one and nothing can hold you back. And you can experience all this even without looking the way you want to. When your self-acceptance is secure, your confidence leads the way. Even if you are unhappy with certain aspects of your appearance, you can still go out and confidently do all the things you want to do. You can be who you want to be. You can finally stop telling yourself, "As soon as I [look better, am thinner, get my wrinkles fixed], I will be able to..."

CONFIDENCE CHANGES EVERYTHING

Several years ago, I was invited to attend an extravagant wedding in Italy. At the time, I was at my heaviest weight, my marriage was at a low point, and I was unhappy with my appearance. I felt conflicted about going to the wedding, but I was curious enough to explore those feelings. I asked myself, *If you were at your most perfect, would you attend this event? What state of mind would you be in? Can you access that state of mind now? Will you have regrets if you don't attend?*

I attended the event and celebrated with my dear friend as she married the man she loves. I chose outfits that made me feel confident and beautiful. I made a conscious decision to come up with two positive comments for each negative comment in my personal thoughts. And I had a wonderful time. It was at this event that I was introduced to the director of a nonprofit arts organization in downtown Portland. She invited me to be on the committee for their upcoming fundraiser. Through that experience, I met the founder of another nonprofit start-up, Gather:Make:Shelter, which serves Portland's houseless community through accountability-based mentorship programs. I was captivated by their mission and the positive changes they were making in the lives of program participants, became involved in their program operations, and am honored to now serve on their board of directors. None of this would have happened if I had allowed how I *felt* about my appearance to rob me of the experience of living.

What would it be like for you to experience that kind of freedom? What would your life be like, and living each day be like, if you could hold that level of self-confidence and acceptance for even a few minutes a day? What would it be like to feel and be beautiful on your terms, according to *your* idea of what is beautiful? If you already experience that, what would it be like to feel it more often? How would it change what you do on a day-to-day basis? What decisions would you make differently?

What would it mean for you *not* to constantly judge yourself and tear at your self-esteem every time you see an image of yourself? What if you could once again—or for the first time—see yourself as beautiful, exactly as you are? Not just because of how you look but because of who you are: the beautiful you, waiting to be experienced.

This is possible. Even if you find yourself thinking, *Yeah, right. Wouldn't that be nice? It may be possible for you, but not for me.*

I hear you. I know such a perspective can seem unattainable. But consider this—it's difficult to imagine yourself having an experience you haven't had before. If you are open to the possibility of feeling the way I have described, it can happen. That is what I want this book to do for you. That is what I want to introduce you to with Thoughtful Aging.

THE FIVE PRINCIPLES
OF THOUGHTFUL AGING

At its simplest, Thoughtful Aging is a more positive approach to aging. It emphasizes personal growth, wisdom, and self-acceptance. It encourages us to reflect on our lives, values, and experiences, helping us to gain a deeper understanding of ourselves and our place in the world.

Thoughtful Aging has five core principles:

- Cultivate a growth mindset

- Embrace curiosity

- Practice self-compassion and acceptance

- Stay mindful and grounded

- Be proactive and responsible

Let's explore each of these in detail.

1. CULTIVATE A GROWTH MINDSET

Thoughtful Aging does not seek to escape aging. It embraces aging. When you shift your thoughts toward embracing the process of aging, you open up so many more possibilities. This is because when you're looking at what you can't do, it's really hard to see what you can do. Aging requires resilience, which we develop by choosing to focus on what can be done rather than on losses or deficits.

If we embrace aging, we can operate from a space of possibility and opportunity rather than a place of scarcity and feeling blocked. We literally cannot see some opportunities and options when we are resisting something or feeling negative about it, much less outright fighting against it. There is clear scientific evidence that our brains can take in more information when we have a positive attitude. A negative attitude, conversely, closes our minds.

I know it can be difficult to feel positive about aging, maybe even impossible in some moments. If you are concerned about how your appearance is changing, or if you are living with conditions such as menopause, sleep problems, weight gain, reduced mobility, or any number of other, more life-threatening health concerns, getting through each day is its own challenge.

It's okay to be honest about not being thrilled with some of the symptoms and experiences of aging. I am not asking you to try to force yourself to be positive about aging. You don't have to love your wrinkles or embrace menopause with open arms. However, an overall positive mindset is critical if you want to see the possibility and opportunity in aging. And as we saw in the last chapter, a lot of what we've been told by society about aging is not true. Many women are happier as they age. But for that to be possible for you, you do have to shift to a positive mindset, even if it's only for a few moments a day at first.

Let me be clear: Thoughtful Aging is not toxic positivity. It doesn't mean pretending that everything is great and ignoring or denying that some truly challenging changes take place as we age. We should not just brush difficult things under the rug because we want to be relentlessly positive all the time or because we are afraid to ask for help. These challenges are a natural part of life.

What we believe makes all the difference. What you believe is reflected back at you when you look in the mirror. When I believed I had "thunder thighs," that's all I saw when I looked in the mirror. I could see nothing else. Outside of the insidious anti-aging culture and societal messaging discussed in the last chapter, changing how you see yourself starts with considering what beliefs you hold and how you came to adopt them. This can have a profound impact on all areas of your life, from how you think of your wrinkles to your relationships to how you participate in your life.

Allow me to borrow the concept of having a "fixed mindset" versus a "growth mindset" from a very popular and impactful book. In *Mindset: The New Psychology of Success,* Stanford psychologist Carol Dweck explains that a fixed mindset assumes we can't change our character, intelligence, or creative abilities in any meaningful way. A growth mindset, on the other hand, thrives on challenges and seeks opportunities for growth. From these two mindsets, which we manifest from a very early age, spring a great deal of our behavior and, ultimately, our capacity for happiness.

If someone lives from a growth mindset, their true potential is unknown (and unknowable) because, in a sense, they have no limits. They have opened the capacity to continue to grow for as long as they live, regardless of what decade they are in. Of course, they will grapple with the same challenges and disappointments that everyone else does. They will have moments of self-doubt, and bad days, and make plenty of mistakes. But all of those experiences are learning experiences for them. They use each one to grow.[15]

Unfortunately, those with a fixed mindset are not so open to growth. They see (and thus experience) challenges as blocks rather than opportunities. They live within limits. They are unable to reimagine and reinterpret themselves, experiences, or situations. This is not their fault. We are not taught in school to use a growth mindset. Some of us may not be lucky enough to interact with people who have a growth mindset. But our ability to shift into a growth mindset is there all the time. We can change how we view the world and how we view ourselves. We do not need money, products, or anything else to make this change. It is available to us right now.

Maybe this sounds a little grand and out of reach. It is not. Remember back in the last chapter when we went over all the research studies and surveys about how women are happier, more confident, and more accepting of how they look as they age? The only real difference between those women and you is their mindset. Because you are reading this book, you most likely have a growth mindset already. Maybe you're not leaping with joy over the prospect of aging, but if you've read even this far, you're open to the idea of loving who you see in the mirror and embracing aging rather than fighting it. You've already grasped the rudiments of having an optimal aging experience. I encourage you to keep going and stay curious. The key to shifting your mindset is becoming curious.

I am having the optimal aging experience. I have never felt more comfortable in my own skin, I no longer worry about what people think. I'm tougher, wiser, and my friendships are better and deeper than ever. Things seem to be getting better with age. Sure, I have a few more wrinkles, but it doesn't really bother me because it feels like a small price to pay for peace of mind. I have made a resolution to focus on the benefits of aging as opposed to the deficits. It seems to be working. I feel as free as if I'm having a second childhood.

—Survey respondent

2. EMBRACE CURIOSITY

Aging, fundamentally, is change. Many people resist change, and for understandable reasons. Change requires adaptation. Adaptation requires effort. If we are already drained and overwhelmed by getting through the basics of living, it can seem hard to find the energy and focus required to adapt to change. We might think, *Things were going along okay before, is this change really necessary? Can I avoid this change? Can I make a few fixes and maybe just deal with it later?*

If you're laughing, that's good. Humor helps, and let's face it: Change is hard. Even when our status quo has been awful, change is still hard. Change requires dealing with unknowns; often, we don't like unknowns. So take all of our natural human resistance to change and fold it into aging and ideas about "losing our beauty," losing our value in society, possibly losing our independence and capabilities, and then eventually dying? Of course we'll resist that. That's scary. But as you saw in the previous chapter, that representation of aging isn't actually true. Women tend to become happier after fifty. With aging comes confidence, wisdom, being authentically yourself, and knowing what matters and doesn't matter in life. That's a pretty good deal in exchange for a few wrinkles.

Focusing on the negative characteristics of aging is responding from a place of fear and resistance. And again, this is a completely human and understandable reaction, especially to something as daunting as aging. But there is another possible response. Change can be met with curiosity. If we take an interest in what is changing without making snap judgments about it, we create an opening for a different interpretation of it.

Curiosity can also be cultivated. It does require us to step away from being fearful, at least a little. But even if we're scared of something, it is possible to teach ourselves to be curious about it. Curiosity is a habit as much as anything, though you will probably need to remind yourself to be curious until the habit becomes ingrained.

Curiosity is the approach that makes possible the growth mindset I mentioned above. You don't even have to adopt an entirely positive attitude to practice curiosity. And it can be practiced in endless tiny ways. You can become curious about anything, like why you put your makeup on in a certain way or the specific routines you follow each day. Or you can explore your relationships—why do you react a certain way in conversations with loved ones, and what shapes those reactions? These moments of curiosity can open the door to greater self-awareness.

I became curious about my body image beliefs after my first child was born. I was so young when I had my son—just eighteen—and no one had told me about the changes my body would go through during pregnancy. I gained a lot of weight. I went from 140 to 175 pounds, with most of the weight gained during my second trimester. My body exploded with stretch marks. I had no idea there were creams and lotions one could use to help skin stretch. As I watched the stretch marks appear seemingly overnight, I didn't realize that they were actually scars that would remain on my body forever. After my son was born, I not only had an unhealthy amount of weight to contend with, but also these new scars all over my abdomen and thighs. I reflected on the times when I thought being a size 10 meant I was "fat." At my new size, 14-plus, I could only dream of being size 10! At that moment, I decided to explore, without pressure, why it was that I struggled to accept my body at any size. This was a years-long process for me, but I eventually found the answers I was seeking.

You can do this, too, but depending on your body image, your body might not be the best place to start. If you need to, start with something less personal. Try looking around at your surroundings. If you are in a familiar room, see if you can notice something about it that you haven't noticed before. Get curious. What would the room look like if you rearranged it? What would it look like if you took something out or added something to it?

If you are around people, this curiosity game gets even better. What is their favorite song? What was the best thing that happened to them this week? Now turn that curiosity inward. Close your eyes, take a deep breath in, let it out, and ask yourself, *What can I do today to grow?* You may need to quiet yourself with more intentional breathing before the answer comes, but it will come. Be curious about the first word that comes to mind.

This tiny little habit of simply practicing curiosity can open everything up. Curiosity about even the most minute experiences and beliefs can carry you all the way to curiosity about new experiences and ideas that you would never have seen or imagined before. This can be done regardless of your age. Curiosity can lead you to learn French at age seventy or win a ballroom dancing competition in your eighties. It might lead you to walk into a music store, buy an instrument you've always wanted to play and schedule your first lesson.

Curiosity can allow you to identify the things you have always wanted to do and then plan to make them happen. It can become a breadcrumb trail of ideas, beliefs, and experiences that create the confidence you've needed to grow, adapt, and learn in ways you never have before. Curiosity will allow your identity to evolve over time so that you can embrace new roles and perspectives that come with aging. It can help you become so much more open to change, which in turn makes it easier to navigate the inevitable transitions that come with aging.

By continuously seeking new experiences and knowledge, we can maintain a sense of purpose and fulfillment, ultimately leading to a more vibrant and satisfying life. Curious people rarely get bored. Even in their nineties and beyond, they have the spark of youthfulness.

> **It is always helpful to hear stories about women my age who are doing fantastic things, be it art, dance, athletics, writing, etc. Also, in retirement you need to recreate yourself. If you had a big career, that was your identity. Your children are now creating lives of their own and it is an ideal time to grow in the areas that interest you, to follow passions that took a back seat to raising a family and handling a career.**
>
> **—Survey respondent**

3. PRACTICE SELF-ACCEPTANCE AND COMPASSION

If I asked you to name all of the things you love, how long would it take you to name yourself? Practicing self-acceptance and self-compassion is lifelong work. As one woman wrote in response to my survey, "Some things are easier to accept than others. It's a daily process of accepting yourself."

Working with issues around appearance and beauty requires ample self-acceptance and self-compassion. Then roll in all the issues, feelings, and implications around aging, and getting to self-acceptance and self-compassion seems even harder. But we don't get there all at once. Getting there takes practice. It is a journey that involves several intentional steps.

The first is to notice how often you compare yourself to others. Seeking connection over comparison enriches our relationships and opens doors to new levels of self-acceptance. By prioritizing meaningful connections, we can celebrate each other's uniqueness rather than struggle to present a polished version of ourselves to keep up with perceived expectations. This shift creates space for deeper conversations, true emotional connection, and a sense of community that is supportive rather than judgmental. There is no need to compare yourself to another. You are perfect just as you are.

The next step is to be careful with yourself. You are your own gatekeeper. Recognize and limit your exposure to people, environments, and media that negatively impact your self-worth or lead to unhealthy comparisons. Toxic or critical people, unrealistic beauty standards, and environments that emphasize superficial values can drain your energy and confidence. I have met many women who seem to always be involved in some sort of drama, only to find out their favorite shows are about drama queen housewives or other reality shows centered around conflict between women. Stepping away from negative influences creates space for positive influences that nurture your growth and reinforce your value as a person, independent of your appearance or societal expectations. If possible, limit your interactions with individuals who make you feel inadequate. Surround yourself with those who uplift and support you, people who value your character and inner qualities. This will reinforce that you are worthy of love and respect just as you are.

Finally, cultivating gratitude for your body shifts the focus from appearance to function and vitality. Rather than concentrating on societal pressures to look a certain way, gratitude invites you to feel a deeper appreciation for what your body can do. It dismantles the harmful effects of body-shaming and objectification by grounding you in the reality that your body is more than a vessel for aesthetics—it is a powerful, resilient entity that supports your well-being. Whether it is the simple joy of walking or the strength to hug a loved one, when you focus on your body's abilities rather than its appearance, you cultivate a healthier, more loving relationship with it.

When I am having a difficult moment with something related to aging, it helps me to remember that aging is a universal experience. Then I treat myself with the same understanding and care I would offer a friend facing similar feelings. Try to talk to yourself the way you would talk to a friend. Almost none of us would ever say the things to a friend that we allow our inner critics to say to ourselves.

> I am accepting who I am and how I show up at any given time in my life. I create a peaceful, healing, supportive, joyful environment to live in and enjoy the freedom to care for my mind, body, and soul.
>
> —Survey respondent

4. STAY MINDFUL AND GROUNDED

Mindfulness practices complement every aspect of Thoughtful Aging. By creating opportunities to be present and undistracted, you can experience your feelings through observation from a nonjudgmental state. This makes self-acceptance easier. It also allows you to see a more complete picture of who you are beyond the negative self-talk.

Mindfulness is where my journey to self-acceptance began. After I had my son, I quickly recognized that having a new baby and working did not leave much time for me. I had to create a space for that curiosity to flourish. I chose to do this in the mornings as I woke up and at night as I fell asleep. This did not come naturally. In my experience, and as I've heard from so many women, anxious thoughts tend to arise just before we fall asleep and after we wake up. We think about what we didn't get done during the day, all the things we think we need to do that day or the next day, money problems, relationship problems, work problems, and basically anything that feels outside of our control.

Have you ever tried to dismiss anxiety? It doesn't work! The thoughts come back louder and stronger. What I've learned is that anxiety is our nervous system's way of trying to protect us from the unknown. In the earliest part of my journey, however, I went through a lot of mental gymnastics as I tried to figure out the magic formula for mindfulness. I realized that if I honored my anxiety by acknowledging it rather than fighting it, accepted that it had a purpose, and thanked it for bringing new things to my awareness, it became much easier to set it aside and quiet my mind. It was during these intentional quiet times, which were not long but consistent, that I learned to reframe my negative body image. My mind would say, *Stretch marks are ugly,* and I would counter that with, *Stretch marks are beautiful. Stretch marks are a privilege to wear.* My mind would say, *You are still so fat,* and I would mentally reply, *You have the power to choose. You are loved.* I made it a rule for myself to reply with two positive statements for each negative statement. Over time, I slowly began to notice my mind becoming freer. I looked forward to my mindfulness moments.

We don't often share our deepest insecurities with others. And I'm not sure that we need to. But it is important to find supportive and positive influences that uplift and affirm you. These are the friends who are not afraid to speak truth in love, allowing you to reflect and course-correct when necessary. Seek professional support, such as therapy or counseling, if you need to work through deeper, lifelong issues around self-esteem and body image.

One of the best results of mindfulness is experiencing grounded presence. If you haven't heard the term before, "grounded presence" simply means staying in the present moment. A grounded presence is similar to mindfulness, but more like a product of mindfulness. Being grounded—as in, uninfluenced by every emotion or thought that passes us by—allows us to hold a balanced and sensible outlook on life, relationships, and aging. This is a true advantage when it comes to Thoughtful Aging. Grounded people are typically present-focused, self-aware, and actively experiencing moments of inner peace. They are well-connected to their environment and emotionally resilient. Who wouldn't want that?

How present or distracted are you in your daily life? No judgment here—we are living in the age of distraction. So much of our lives are spent worrying about the future or replaying the past; being grounded and present is an increasingly rare experience for many people. But a grounded presence fosters stability, resilience, and a deeper connection with oneself and others. It is from this space that we can stay present and fully engaged in the moment. This can help mitigate the anxiety and stress that often accompany aging-related changes and uncertainties.

So, how do we get grounded? There are many ways, and what works for one person may not work for you. You may also have to try a few different things to learn what works for you. Again, being grounded means being present in each moment. It also means being anchored in a way of life that is internally driven. You become grounded by developing a foundation for your existence based on a set of internal values and principles that guide your behavior, decision-making, and overall approach to life.

Are you longing for a sense of contentment and well-being? Get grounded. Do you wish to stay regulated in stressful situations? Get grounded. Feeling emotional all the time? Get grounded. A grounded presence enhances emotional regulation, giving us more ability to navigate the ups and downs of aging. It supports and is supported by mindfulness and self-awareness, allowing us to further deconstruct our negative self-talk and feelings of being "less than" or "other" without becoming overwhelmed by them.

As I experienced body changes during and after pregnancy, I felt both "less than" and "other" when it came to redefining my place in the world. While I was caring for a newborn, friends my age were attending college and had lives that revolved around whatever it was they wanted to do. My life had departed so drastically from what I thought it would be that I couldn't help but feel left out. I couldn't afford to go out and I did not have the freedom to attend social gatherings. I also found the distance growing between my friends and me because I could no longer relate to them, nor they to me; I was surviving on WIC vouchers and food stamps while they were getting college degrees.

I began to incorporate mindfulness moments into my day by consciously choosing positive thoughts. I turned finding the "silver lining" into a game. If a thought or situation arose that left me feeling unsteady (ungrounded),

I reminded myself of all the things in my life for which I could be grateful. At times, it was as basic as *At least I have a roof over my head* or *We have food to eat and many people don't. We're okay.* This may seem extreme, but I was determined not to fall into despair as the feelings of being "less than" and "other" tried to creep in. Cultivating mindfulness allowed me to stay grounded and handle life's ups and downs with more clarity and strength.

Staying in the present moment did not happen by accident for me, and it will not for you. It requires intentionally disrupting the chaotic frequencies to which we have become accustomed. Meditation, breathwork, connecting with nature, conversations with God, music, physical activity, and visualization can all be useful guides to finding what works for you. For many, something as simple as establishing a daily routine can create a sense of order and predictability. The goal is to create moments throughout the day when you connect mind and body to be fully present. We can do this more successfully if we listen to our bodies from a place of partnership rather than limitation or control. I will talk about this a great deal in later chapters.

Note, too, that what grounds us at one stage of our lives may not necessarily work for us in other stages. This is especially true during life's transitions. If you are not getting quite the same amount of comfort from certain practices as you used to, it may be time to invoke a bit of curiosity and self-acceptance so you can try new things.

> **I know aging is a natural process. I actually enjoy evolving and becoming more and more who I was meant to be, embracing where I am every day in my journey and accepting what is. So I know my appearance is what I choose it to be.**
>
> **—Survey respondent**

5. BE PROACTIVE AND RESPONSIBLE

Proactivity and responsibility are helpful for all aspects of successful aging, but they are essential in matters of health. Taking proactive steps toward guarding and cultivating your health is one of the best investments you can make in yourself. You alone are accountable for your health. Do not rely on doctors to tell you everything you need to know, or even to recognize when you need something. In a sense, *you* are your primary care provider.

One young woman I spoke with found a painful lump in her breast when she was twenty-four. She had been unusually tired and really felt like something wasn't right, so she made an appointment with her gynecologist and was seen the following month. Given her young age, her doctor suggested it was likely related to her monthly cycle, although she had shared other symptoms that wouldn't usually be associated with a reproductive issue. Though no tests were taken, she was sent home with instructions to return if the pain didn't stop. The doctor reassured her that it was likely nothing to worry about.

The pain didn't stop. By the time she could get another appointment to be checked and have a biopsy scheduled, two more months had gone by. She was diagnosed with stage 4 breast cancer and began a long-term chemotherapy treatment plan that wreaked havoc on her body. Though her doctor was finally taking her seriously, she had still been incorrectly diagnosed. It turned out that her dismissed lump was a complex combination of conditions. She actually had an autoimmune disease that mimicked cancer along with an earlier-stage breast cancer. Upon reviewing her medical records, she discovered that the autoimmune disease had been suspected but never explored, and once chemotherapy began, they were unable to test for it. Had she been tested before starting her chemotherapy treatment, her treatment plan would likely have been a mix of medications for the autoimmune disease and surgery with radiation for the breast cancer. In the end, she did have surgery and not only lost one of her breasts but all of the lymph nodes in her left arm as well.

Many of us have our own such story or have heard the story of another whose symptoms were dismissed by a medical provider, only to find out later that a problem did exist. It is basic pragmatism to recognize that the older we get, the more support our bodies will need. The more we learn to listen to our bodies, the more confident we will become as advocates for our own health. We can support our own aging by responding to what our body needs and learning our body's language.

By taking responsibility for your well-being, you can direct your care in a way that aligns with your long-term aging goals. You have resources such as doctors, nutritionists, medical experts, alternative care providers, and innumerable online pages of information at your fingertips. Advocating for your own needs, asking for help when you need it, building a medical team of professional longevity providers committed to working *with* you and staying informed will help you maintain your long-term health and happiness. Be proactive, seek preventive care, and make lifestyle changes that support your well-being.

These five principles of Thoughtful Aging will get you a long way toward both loving who you see in the mirror and having an optimal aging experience. Applied together and consistently, they address all aspects of our lives—our minds, bodies, and souls. They allow us to connect with the people we love and find purpose and meaning at any stage of life. Exactly how they are applied, however, is up to you. Just as the fifth principle, "Be proactive and responsible," implies, you are in charge of your care. I won't tell you what to do anywhere in this book. Instead, I'll share principles and examples, leaving you the space to decide what works best for your journey.

> *What would you need to know, do, have, or be to achieve that vision of your optimal aging?*
>
> **I would need to stay educated about healthy living and then take action. I believe you have to be intentional about achieving that vision.**
>
> **—Survey question and respondent answer**

Chapter 3:

Authenticity, Expectations, and Our Need to Belong

What we think about our appearance is intrinsically linked to how we feel about ourselves. If we're going to change how we feel about how we look, we must shift the narrative about what we see in the mirror. We want our focus to go from finding things to "fix" toward honoring what is.

So far, I've exposed the flaws of anti-aging as a mindset and as an industry. Then I explained how the industry, media, and advertising are really just taking their cues from societal beliefs. In the last chapter, I introduced the principles of Thoughtful Aging. Now, let's dive into how the story we tell ourselves when we look in the mirror is shaped from the very beginning.

FINDING OUR WAY
IN AN IMPERFECT WORLD

You were born perfectly—mind, body, and soul—into an imperfect world. Stop for a moment and let that sink in. This isn't about being flawless—it's about recognizing that your arrival here, in your specific body, mind, and soul, was no accident. The circumstances you were born into, however imperfect they may seem, were exactly as they were meant to be.

You are meant to be here. There is no one on this planet who doesn't belong, and that includes you. Sometimes, it may feel like you were born into the wrong family or the wrong situation. But that's not true. You were born into your circumstances for a reason. Whether you felt out of place or not, you belonged exactly where you were.

The key is understanding that we have the power to shape our lives within the circumstances we're given. That's where autonomy comes in—we get to decide what we want to do with this gift of life.

But under no circumstances should you ever believe that you don't belong. You do. Even if the family or situation you were born into feels like a poor fit, you were always meant to be part of this world. You may not always fit into the world's expectations, but you always belong.

The moment you took your first breath, you became dependent upon your caregivers to guide you through the beautiful chaos of this world. Here's the problem, though: They didn't fully understand what was best for you. They didn't—and couldn't—know what your soul was meant to express. Your caregivers arrived in this world the same way. They, too, were dependent on their caregivers for guidance, and they on theirs, and so on back through the generations. Can you see the problem this creates? Your soul, and your life, were meant to be experienced and lived through you, according to your own unique inner calling. While your caregivers may have meant well, they could not truly know what your unique path and purpose were meant to be. How could they? Only you know the song your soul was meant to sing. In an effort to help you navigate life, they created rules for you to follow, often based on rules they were taught or learned through religious principles, survival, idealism, conformity, and safety.

Your soul, with the help of your conscience, integrated the values contained within those rules to form your identity. This all happened without your conscious knowledge as you learned to navigate a complicated world. It occurred when you were a child, before you had the insight to determine what was truly right for you.

There comes a point for all of us when what we believe is right or wrong comes into conflict with what we were *taught* to believe is right or wrong. As a child or young adult, you didn't have much choice. You could choose conformity and maintain a sense of belonging, or choose integrity and risk being judged, ridiculed, or even cast out.

Think back to a time when you were pressured to fit in with a group, maybe in high school or at work. Imagine a situation where everyone around you was gossiping about someone and you felt the pull to join in just to belong. Deep down, though, you knew it was wrong. Maybe you felt an uneasy knot in your stomach, knowing it was not how you wanted to treat others. In that moment, you had a choice: go along with the group to maintain your sense of belonging or stand in your integrity and risk being judged or excluded.

Choosing conformity will allow you to blend in, feel accepted, and avoid conflict. But choosing integrity—speaking up instead of staying silent—might make you a target for judgment. It's not always easy to do what's right, but your inner sense, the part of you that recognizes right from wrong, guides you. This discernment may push you outside of the rules and guidelines created for you by others.

As an adult, you now have the power to make decisions based on what your soul knows to be right, even if it means standing alone. It's in that space, where you trust your own voice, that Thoughtful Aging begins to flourish.

A vital component of Thoughtful Aging is realizing your limitless options. This is part of the growth mindset principle we talked about in the last chapter. With a growth mindset, you can choose to create the song your soul was meant to sing, or you can continue to play the tune you were taught to play. So, ask yourself: Are you happy with the melody of your life? If not, what would you change?

OUR NEED TO BELONG

I have always longed for connection. It's the heartbeat of my soul. I married young, guided by a sense of duty and the weight of religious standards that shaped much of my upbringing. At eighteen, I became a mother for the first time. By age twenty-two, I had three beautiful children. I felt a connection with these three tiny little people that was unlike anything I had ever experienced. They offered me constant love, as children do when they are young, which furthered my desire for deep connection. *They needed me. I felt loved. I had a purpose.* On the surface, it seemed like I was building a life, but inside, I felt a familiar disconnect—a gap between who I thought I was supposed to be and who I felt I really was.

My marriage, though well-intentioned, fell apart after six years. My husband's choice of addiction over family left me navigating single motherhood while working two jobs. The challenges of raising three children on my own were enough to distract me from the realization that somewhere along the way, I'd lost sight of myself. I felt as if there were parts of me I had yet to discover, but I had no time or skills to do so. I found my mind wandering to the past in an effort to understand the present.

Growing up, perfection was always the goal—an unspoken expectation that hovered over everything I did.

Mixed messages of "you are loved, yet not good enough" shaped me in ways I couldn't quite untangle. I became a people-pleaser, constantly adjusting who I was to fit the mold of what was expected. I avoided conflict like the plague. This left me feeling like a shell of myself, going through the motions but never truly connecting with the life I was living. My attempts to push back at expectations were met with anger, rejection, and fear-based threats.

Dr. Gabor Maté, a renowned Canadian physician, speaker, and author who is widely recognized for his work in addiction, trauma, and mind-body health, says that humans have two emotional needs: self-expression and belonging.[16] When the two needs clash, we often choose a sense of belonging over self-expression. When we do this, we devalue ourselves and find ourselves further from the truth. Each people-pleasing, conflict-avoidant step I took led me further away from the song my soul was meant to sing.

Pushing back against other people's ideas of what we should want and what we should do can be hard. I know this from experience, as does almost every other woman with whom I have spoken. Often it means challenging people we love to accept us for who we are, not who they want us to be. We're asking them to grow with us, at least enough to see us in new ways. We're asking them to change, even if it's just a little bit. That can put pressure on our relationships. In some cases, we risk losing friends and family members who are unwilling to accept us for who we are and who we are becoming.

We all want to be loved. We want to be seen for who we are. We have a genetic need to belong. The idea of risking relationships for the sake of internal alignment may sound scary. After all, operating within the safety zone is much more predictable. What I learned, and what I hope you can realize, is that you will be uncomfortable either way. Living by another's standards for the sake of belonging creates incredible discomfort. Challenging those standards through action produced by self-discovery can also create discomfort. The difference is, one keeps you suppressed and the other is a path to freedom and full self-expression. Also, how can we expect to be loved, accepted, and seen for who we authentically are if we haven't embodied a lifestyle of self-discovery and full expression? In other words, people only see what we allow them to see. We cannot relate to others beyond the depth we have reached within ourselves. We cannot express our full beauty unless we truly know ourselves.

FROM OBLIGATION TO AUTHENTICITY

For a long time, I only allowed people to see a very limited version of me. I felt alone and unworthy of anything other than the isolated single-mother life I had adopted as my new identity. I found myself withdrawing and not pursuing new friendships because I didn't feel like I could measure up. I looked at other women and assumed they had it all figured out—that they were comfortable in their own skin and had it all together. I was sure they could never relate to the challenges of my day-to-day life.

The truth is, we're all struggling in some way, but it's hard to remember that when you're caught up in your own insecurities.

I missed out on innumerable opportunities to feel supported and learn from others because I had only ever been taught to endure. What I did learn during that time is that enduring is surviving, not thriving. There is a quiet confidence in knowing and expressing our truth that shifts us from enduring life to engaging with life. It was several years before I realized that having the ability to endure is a desirable skill but not a final destination. Once I began my soul journey of self-discovery through reflection, therapy, and practicing vulnerability, a deep desire to see others and be seen by them became a driving force in my life. But first I had to figure out who I was and how I came to be.

We do whatever we need to do to fit into our particular communities and groups. The question is, how many of the messages and unwritten rules of our families, social circles, and communities can we embody and still be ourselves?

The messages from our families, particularly our mothers, are deeply ingrained. They shape our understanding of beauty, success, and what it means to be a woman. Our social circles reinforce these ideals with unspoken rules about appearance, behavior, and status, dictating how we should present ourselves to the world. These communities often value conformity and leave little room for deviation from the norm. Like many others, I learned to navigate these expectations by adopting them as my own, believing that doing so was the key to acceptance and belonging. This was not only exhausting but unsustainable.

As I became aware of the messages I had internalized, my desire to live authentically took root. I began to question which of these unwritten rules truly served me and which were merely constructs I had accepted without examination. I understood that while some values and traditions from my family and community were meaningful and worth preserving, others were based on outdated ideals that did not align with my evolving sense of self.

The key for me was in discerning where these external influences ended and where my true self began. I sought the help of a therapist, Peggy Senger Parsons, whose writings and advocacy for those less fortunate have left a global fingerprint on this world. I consider her my first true mentor. She is a Quaker minister, which was a giant leap into the lion's den for me. Talk about pushing back! The religion in which I was raised had led me to believe that women could and should not hold leadership positions within the church.

Seeking a therapist, much less a woman minister, was about as religiously rebellious as I could be. But there I was, taking my first step toward self-discovery and alignment. I embraced curiosity and, with Peggy's help, I learned that it was possible to honor my family and community without being entirely defined by them. I could respect my parents' values and the social norms of my circles, but I didn't have to let them dictate every aspect of my life. Instead, I began to selectively embody the aspects of these messages that resonated with me while letting go of those that did not.

I found that being myself didn't mean completely rejecting my upbringing or my social context; it meant integrating the parts that felt authentic and discarding the rest. This process required introspection and the courage to stand apart when necessary. I learned to set boundaries, say no to the expectations that didn't serve me, and embrace the parts of myself that had been overshadowed by the need to conform.

I continued therapy with Peggy for several years, discovering that the messages and unwritten rules of my family, social circles, and communities could coexist with my true self, but only to the extent that they aligned with my own values and identity. I realized that I didn't have to completely embody these external expectations to be accepted or loved. By finding this balance, I was able to reclaim a sense of self and live in a way that was both true to my roots and authentic to my own spirit.

The relationship between our authenticity and the needs of those around us evolves continuously. It can shift even daily, shaped by the many small decisions we make. Navigating the space between ourselves, our loved ones, and our communities is a dynamic process. Yet it's within these contradictions that we develop discernment, a key aspect of energy balance. As the saying attributed to Bruce Lee goes: "Absorb what's useful, discard what's not, add what is uniquely your own."[17]

When we find ourselves in a new phase of life, it's an excellent opportunity to look back at where we have been and ask ourselves: *How can I begin to reintegrate the things I truly wanted to do, but felt I couldn't, into the person I am today?* Sometimes it means letting go of ideas with which you no longer align, as I did when I re-examined my belief that women should not hold pastoral roles. Sometimes it means coming back to values and actions that are genuine and authentic to you. This is what it takes to write the song your soul was meant to sing.

If you feel especially uncertain about what is authentic to you and what you really love, think about what you loved as a child. What things, places, and activities did you enjoy most when you were a child? Was it working with animals? Having conversations with elderly people? Functional problem-solving? Trust your intuition. It will tell you what is right and wrong, good and bad—for you. It will show you what to say and when to say it. If you're focused on being centered and in alignment, then whatever you say or do will come from a good place. There are a multitude of blessings just waiting for those who can find beauty in both the past and present.

THE KEY TO EMBRACING CHANGE

The women I've met through working in aesthetics come in because they are looking for change. They are trying to find their way back to themselves. An obvious first step is enhancing their appearance to more accurately reflect how they feel on the inside. They are taking steps to figure out that balance between their current life and social circumstances and the person they feel they really are, or want to be, on the inside.

This is a worthwhile pursuit, but it can present challenges. When we pursue change, it disrupts who we've been. And when we change, the people in our lives may not be able to adapt. They have grown accustomed to us being a certain way. Our change disrupts their view of us, and that can disrupt their view of themselves. If they aren't used to or aren't prepared for having their view of themselves disrupted, it can be terrifying; us changing can be threatening to them, so they may push back against our changes with suppressive and limiting comments. They may question why we've changed or even why we would want to change.

Facing this judgment from others may cause us to question our choices, especially if we're not entirely confident in our changing selves. But consider this: You can only feel judgment from others if you are judging yourself. Stop for a moment and think of the last time you felt judged by someone for something you said or did. My guess is that your first response was to question your worth, wonder if you had said or done something wrong, or immediately internalize a negative thought.

Having the wherewithal to withstand judgment or criticism for changing requires a willingness to explore insecurities. Judgment plays on insecurities. The more confident you become, the less insecure you feel. The less insecure you feel, the more easily you can walk the path toward self-acceptance. Radical self-acceptance is your armor against feeling judged for who you are or how you present yourself in the world. If you're not feeling it now, don't worry. You can get there. This character trait can be developed.

When you are ready, begin by exploring who you are and who you want to be from a character-based viewpoint. This means focusing on your personal values, integrity, and moral compass rather than external achievements, status, and material success. It involves assessing your inner qualities—such as honesty, compassion, resilience, and responsibility—and considering how you want to develop these traits over time.

Rather than asking questions like *What do I want to have?* or *How do I want to be seen?* the focus shifts to *Who am I at my core?* and *What kind of person do I want to become?* It's about aligning your actions with your values and making choices that reflect the type of character you wish to cultivate, guided by principles that lead to your fulfillment and authenticity. Do this and the ground you're standing on becomes solid. It's been defined by you, determined by you, and accepted by you. That is the launchpad for change and growth. Remember, only you know you. If you are earnestly seeking ways to operate at a higher frequency, you will find them.

When you approach change from that viewpoint, any decision you make is in alignment because you have already decided that it is. You have the strength of character to withstand any judgment from others—real or perceived—because you are on solid ground. You are aligned and recalibrated. You are genuine and authentic to your soul, heart, mind, body, who you are as a person, and how you wish to present yourself in the world.

Without that, you can't get to the new version of yourself. You remain externally driven and have no footing; you just blow with the wind. Any new trend that comes along leads you in a new direction.

Big eyebrows are a perfect example. Back in the '90s and 2000s, the trend was to make your eyebrows so thin you could barely see them. Prior to that, actresses like Grace Kelly and Elizabeth Taylor had set the standard for big, beautiful, well-groomed, prominent eyebrows. Once the trend of thin eyebrows took hold, some women went so far as to shave them off and draw them in. Do you know anyone who fell victim to this trend? I say "fell victim to" because I can't tell you the number of women with whom I've spoken who would give anything to have their eyebrows return to their natural state. You see, they did not realize at the time that they were forever altering their appearance. The wisdom of age has taught them that you don't need to follow every beauty trend—or any trend—to feel good about yourself. In fact, following a particular trend today might be detrimental to your future self. Too often, we do not consider our future selves in today's decisions and end up in places we don't want to be.

HOW HELEN EMBRACED
HER FUTURE SELF

I met Helen at the clinic when she stopped in to purchase sunscreen. She shared with me that she had lost more than a hundred pounds over the previous two years and had kept the weight off. When I asked what diet program she had followed, she said, "None. I woke up one day and realized how unhealthy I was. I realized how limited I had become in what I could do and what I thought about my future self. I then had a conversation with my future self about what changes I would need to make today to honor her. That led to me changing my eating habits and gradually increasing my activity levels. Each day I would have a conversation with my future self, and each day my cravings became less and less. I'm proud of what I've accomplished because it was done from a place of honor, not restriction."

I love everything about this. Helen was a woman facing seemingly insurmountable health issues who bucked convention and found a way to reclaim her health in a way that was genuine and authentic to her. It is important to note that this solution was not handed to her. She actively pursued a deeper understanding of herself from a place of accountability, not judgment. This gave her the liberty to get curious, draw on her own strength as a resource, and stand confidently in front of the mirror having achieved an incredible milestone. She gave the gift of health to her future self.

Why we do the things we do is at the heart of the decisions that we make. Far too often, the desire to fit in and be accepted by others overshadows our desire to live in alignment with our values and principles. We have an opportunity to return to our true selves. We can rediscover our beauty—our very own soul song—and share it confidently with the world around us.

To accomplish this usually requires a change in how we see and understand ourselves. But we need to change how we see and understand beauty, too.

My aunt Sherry was this way. She was the kind of person who radiated self-acceptance and joy, a living example of what it means to be in alignment with one's true self. Her home was a place I could go to experience laughter and joy. She did not meet conventional beauty standards by any means—she was overweight, had a gap between her front teeth, and her hair was dry and overprocessed. Despite living alone, she was the happiest person I knew and freely shared her joy with those she invited into her life. She had vibrant friendships, many with people she met while working as a restaurant manager. During her eighteen-year career, she mentored hundreds of employees, offering them guidance and support through their life transitions. She felt most beautiful when she accessorized her outfits with jewelry she had purchased for herself. I admired how she embraced her beauty. I never once heard her say anything negative about herself. And being in her vibrant presence was comforting. When you are in the presence of someone who is happy with who they are and the beauty they possess, it is much easier to feel it within yourself.

Chapter 4:

Reflections Beyond the Surface

Beauty is a multifaceted thing, and women's beauty is even more so. Who and what we see in the mirror is not static. Our faces change over time, but how we see ourselves changes as well.

Our image in the mirror can reassure us, evoke pride, or be an unwelcome reminder of damaged self-esteem. How we feel about ourselves is reflected in what we see. We can look at the same face, in the same setting, on the same day, and see any of those aspects. Sometimes, we can almost see them all at once—in a face that makes us feel proud and grounded despite our insecurity about wrinkles and jowls.

What we see is entirely up to us. We choose what we see and how we see ourselves, whether we're aware of it or not. Too often, though, we choose to view ourselves through the unhelpful messaging of the anti-aging industry, society, or an ad we saw on Instagram last night.

Not much in life is truly within our control (how people act, what's on the news, even what happens over the course of a day, for example), but we can choose how we see ourselves. We can choose to see our beauty. For some of us, this can be challenging—especially for women who are trained, as we are, to scan our images for faults, "problem areas," or any possible sign of something that needs to be "fixed."

REFRAME THAT NEW WRINKLE

Imagine approaching your bathroom mirror tomorrow morning just after you wake up. You see a wrinkle you had not noticed before. There it is, just above your eyebrow. The angle of the light falling on your bathroom mirror is accentuating it.

How will you respond to this wrinkle? Will you react to it instantly as a negative thing? Will you schedule a treatment to remove it? Will you "fix" it, or will you apply some curiosity and have another response?

You could pause for a moment and assess how you really feel about this wrinkle. Is it a marker that proclaims you are growing older, that time is passing rapidly while you are caught up in the day-to-day scramble? Does it make you wonder if you are using the time you've been given well? Are you doing things that are meaningful to you, or things that you feel others expect you to do?

Does this wrinkle make you worry that you are not as attractive as you once were? Does it create concern that your partner might not find you as attractive, or that you are not going to look as good on camera? Does it make you worry about being sidelined at work? Or that people will think you are angry? Or are you not actually bothered by this wrinkle at all but simply reacting to it because that is the way you've been conditioned to respond after decades of messaging from the anti-aging industry and society at large?

Could you see this wrinkle differently? What if it is a mark of the difficult year you just navigated, one you got through with dignity and grace? What if you developed it from laughing, or smiling? Or maybe it came from frowning because you've been caring for an older parent, or helping one of your children through a divorce, or going through your own divorce, or supporting your partner through a career change. This wrinkle may have happened because you care deeply about the people in your life and support them as best you can. Or what if this wrinkle is a sign that you could use a good, long, real rest before a health event forces you to rest?

Considering all that, perhaps you don't want to "fix" the wrinkle. What will happen if you decide you want to keep it? What if you rather like the look of yourself as an experienced, wise woman who loves and lives fully?

If you can get past the anti-aging messaging and insecurities about not being loved, seen, respected, or included because of your age, then it is truly your choice to address this wrinkle in any way you see fit. Your decision becomes one of want and not need. If you *need* to have this wrinkle removed, then you are not making a choice. You are being pressured by the anti-aging industry and what you think other people expect of you.

WHAT WOMEN SEE IN THE MIRROR

This question of what we see when we look in the mirror is so important that I asked the women I surveyed about it. Here is how they answered the question, "What do you think about or notice when you look in the mirror and see signs of aging?"

I asked this as an open-ended question expressly because I wanted to know what women had to say about this in their own words. The answers they gave reflected the two primary ways women see themselves and the way our culture recognizes beauty: they focus on the surface, or they look deeper.

About half of the women who answered this question mentioned specific external faults—jowls, dark circles, etc. Most women noticed negative things about themselves; only about one in four of them said they saw something positive.

Answers like "Don't like it," "Don't recognize self," and "Sad" made up over 10% of the responses. The action-oriented response of "Do something" to "Fix" themselves accounted for over 10% of the answers.

The comments women made in response to this question reflect a wide variation of experience, but there are definite trends.

Some of the responses are quite dark:

- *I look in the mirror and cry.*

- *I want to die.*

- *I think, oh my God, I am my mother's daughter. I'm getting old. And then I usually cry for a minute and have an anxiety attack.*

- *It makes me extremely sad and self-conscious.*

- *Despair.*

- *Hate.*

- *Scared.*

In some of the responses, women talk about how ugly they feel. This is heartbreaking. These are the hardest comments to read. To see yourself as ugly speaks to a level of self-hatred no one should have to bear.

- *I'm getting uglier every day.*

- *I have always been ugly.*

- *When I look in the mirror, I try not to cry because I find the person I see ugly and am told by the person I chose in life that I am, too.*

- *I think that I look awful and hate how I look.*

Several women contemplate death and the end of life in what they see:

- *I don't want to get old. I don't want to die.*

- *I worry about how much time I have left with my kids.*

- *Death. I notice that I'm no longer in my thirties. My teeth are gone and my face has changed shape. I see a rendition of a 1950s wicked witch.*

Many women simply wonder about where the time has gone, or what meaning their life has had:

- *How did this happen? Life goes by faster than you think, so enjoy it as long as you can.*

- *How much of my life has slipped away without my having done anything meaningful enough.*

- *I wonder what I have done in my life that gave it purpose.*

Many women do not recognize themselves. They describe a sense of a loss of identity:

- *I think that I don't look like myself. I see myself more as how I looked when I was younger and then I look in the mirror and sometimes I'm surprised by what I see.*

- *Where did me go?*

- *I get really bad anxiety because I feel like my face is what makes me.*

- *My skin has changed a lot! I have age spots, skin tags, and have to work hard to keep my cheeks up to smile. It's shocking to me because in my dreams I always see myself as the younger me. So to wake up and see this fifty-something lady staring back is daunting at times.*

- *When I notice signs of aging every time I look at myself, I kind of cringe. I don't like to age and I want to continue to look younger than I am. A lot of times I just see somebody tired looking back at me.*

- *I don't recognize myself.*

- *Who is that in the mirror!!!!???*

Some say they feel a great difference between how they feel and how they look:

- *Sometimes I don't recognize myself. There is a disconnect between how I feel and how I look.*

- *How I feel thirty-five but look fifty-four... it's sometimes hard to adjust the brain to the body.*

- *I devalue myself. I want to hide. I want to get plastic surgery. I just want my outside to match what I feel I look like inside.*

- *WHY?!?! The face doesn't always reflect how I feel inside. Feeling good, strong, positive, and then you wonder who that older person is staring at you.*

- *I notice my eyes and the skin around them. I notice a heaviness I don't want, like a gravity heaviness. I just want to continue to look like myself—I'm fine with looking older, I just want to feel like the outside matches who I feel like inside.*

Others describe a pervasive, even profound tiredness or dullness:

- *My eyes look tired. There's no spark in my eyes.*
- *How old I look and how my skin looks so terrible. My sunken eyes and years of pain.*
- *I just think about how stressful everything is.*
- *I see myself looking tired pretty much all the time.*
- *Blah skin. No glow.*

A few women actively try not to look in the mirror:

- *I don't want to have a mirror around me anymore.*
- *I don't use mirrors if I can avoid them.*
- *I don't/can't look in the mirror these last few years. My entire life, starting in high school and up until the past few years, my experience was the same and got worse as time went on: all I could*

see was something or plural somethings on my face and/or body that I deemed unacceptable and I would fixate, problem-solve, research how to change it/make it better.

Some are spurred to take better care of themselves:

- *I think wow I look terrible. I need to go get something done.*

- *I need to take care of myself better.*

- *I need to focus on my health.*

- *I wish I knew how to fix my skin issues and how I need to take care of myself before everyone else.*

- *I see a lot of aging, including fine lines and thinning skin, and I get frustrated with myself for not putting in the work for proper skin care when I'm tired.*

Many wonder how they are perceived by others:

- *I wonder how other people see me. Do they think I'm younger or older than I actually am?*

- *I see sad eyes looking back at me and hope I look better to other people.*

- *People are superficial and I have to fix up to get any type of respect when dealing with the general public.*

Some simply miss how they used to look:

- *I wish I were as pretty as I was when I was younger.*

- *I miss my neck.*

- *I notice shadows in my chin area that are more pronounced. I'm seeing fine lines deepen as I age and my cheeks not being as full. It makes me miss who I was and want to seek out treatments to restore how I feel I should look.*

But some, despite seeing things they don't like, have a sense of humor about it all:

- *I don't see much because my eyesight is also getting worse. Ha.*

- *Weird goat hairs that suddenly sprout from my chin? AM I part goat? Was I cursed by someone to become part goat?*

- *I must admit, I don't love it. But I don't have acne anymore—that's a plus.*

- *I think that I look great still as long as I don't look too close. Is that okay?*

Some recognize that aging is inevitable, but they still struggle with seeing its effects in the mirror:

- *I look old... I need to get more Botox. I wish I could afford more filler. Maybe it's just bad lighting. Oh well... Still working on the acceptance and being grateful part ;)*

- *It's sad... I try to think of it as time passing with beautiful memories and experiences but it's still really hard.*

- *It's difficult... It's difficult to keep that positive self-talk. In some ways, I see how for my age I have worked hard to maintain a decent appearance and self-care, but it's still hard to look in the mirror and acknowledge that that youth is gone.*

- *Scared! But trying to embrace life's stages.*

Then there are the positive comments.

Many women do still see themselves when they look in the mirror:

- *I still see a beautiful me. STILL SEE ME. I see the older version of ME.*

Many also see the arc of their lives, but in a positive light:

- *I like me and I have been through it and still like me. Strong woman.*

- *I wear it well. It reminds me of everything I've been through in my life.*

- *I think about the life I've lived.*

- *I have experienced life and I am not superficial. Being happy with who I am is a great achievement in life. You have to let go of what others may say.*

- *I accept the reality of what I see and am grateful for health and well-being.*

- *I've had a wonderful life so far.*

- *I think of all the fun memories I've had.*

- *All that I have been through, as if I'm looking at a photo album. I think about what another forty years will create on my skin and body and how I want that to be shaped by what I can control.*

Many recognize the gift of being able to age at all:

- *I think how lucky I am to be alive each day. I get to play with my rescued dog and do whatever I want.*

- *Better than the alternative.*

- *That I'm beautiful and I'm still here on earth.*

- *I am proud to be alive and able to do what I want to do.*

- *I'm getting older and it's a beautiful thing. I'm still alive. I know people who haven't made it to my age or past it.*

- *I'm happy. It's a blessing to be able to age. Not many people are blessed with that.*

- *I think wow, I'm a badass and a survivor.*

- *I think I'm lucky to be alive so I'm not going to get down about aging. Aging is a gift.*

- *Happy that I'm alive and can enjoy the changes in my body.*

Though I would like there to be more of them, quite a few women do see their beauty:

- *I used to notice my sagging jawline and expression wrinkles on my forehead but now I look into my eyes and check for my sparkle. I still have it!*

- *I think I look great!!!*

- *I think I have aged gracefully so it doesn't really bother me.*

- *I think that I look great at my age.*

- *Beauty and grace.*

- *At first I think, "OMG I LOOK OLD." But then, almost instantly, I think, "Hey, I look pretty good for as old as I am." I look pretty good for ANY age.*

- *I love my long silver-gray hair!*

- *I'm starting to look more and more like my mother. But that's okay, my mother was a beautiful woman and so am I.*

- *Aging can be beautiful. You will change in appearance, accept it.*

- *I notice gray hair and a beautiful woman who's becoming the woman she's supposed to be.*

- *Beauty.*

- *That I'm beautiful by my own standards and not anyone else's.*

- *I think I am beautiful. I do not buy shoes, I buy skin products. When I find something that is working, I stick with it until it is no longer satisfying my skin needs.*

- *I love what I see.*

- *Beautiful still.*

And some see a mix of good and bad, depending on the day:

- *Some days I'm okay with it, some days I love it and some days I want to go back thirty years.*

- *Sometimes I look tired... sometimes I look really damn good!*

- *Depends on the day. Sometimes I feel like I look old. Sometimes I think I'm aging gracefully.*

- *I'm happy with what I see most of the time. I would like to reduce sun damage and wrinkles. Since starting injectables last year, I feel it has made a difference.*

Some see room for improvement:

- *I think there is some honor in aging, that we've lived long enough to have wrinkles and be part of the older generation. I do see things I want to improve though, mostly about my muscle tone and being more physically fit.*

- *That I'm getting older and there is nothing I could do to stop it but at least try to make sure I'm as healthy as possible.*

- *That I do not look too bad, but I would like to do some things that would help.*

- *I understand it's the cycle of life, but also believe what I do to take care of myself is a key in this.*

- *How to get happier to look better.*

- Some are satisfied enough with their looks:

- *I think I look good.*

- *I still look pretty darn good!*

- *I don't like to see the slight sagging skin on my upper arms or face. Other than that, I think I've aged pretty well.*

- *I look in the mirror and I say, "Hi Mom!" Lol. I'd like to take off this weight. It's really uncomfortable. The rest? Gray hair, slight wrinkles, etc. I'm fine with it. I'm not supposed to look twenty-five forever.*

- *I actually look pretty good, with the help of Botox, etc.*

- *I think I look pretty good for fifty-two.*

- *Sun spots, wrinkles, gray hair, but I think ultimately, it's okay. I'm fifty-eight. I smile.*

- *It bothers me to a certain extent. But I have given in to seeing my hair gray. I kind of like it. Since I am retired, I can see that I am much more rested compared to earlier in my life when I worked.*

- *I am on the right track. I am doing well with my skin regimen.*

- *I don't worry much about the aging signs. I am happy with my life and as much as I can still do.*

And some see wisdom:

- *I see myself older and I hope wiser.*

- *I look in the mirror and see wisdom.*

As you can see, looking in the mirror—really looking—is not an exercise for the fainthearted. In myths and storytelling, looking in the mirror is presented as an evaluation of self. Sometimes it is a reckoning, a test of one's character. How we see ourselves speaks volumes about our identity. For many, it is their identity.

That's why it is so interesting that approximately half of the women I surveyed look in the mirror and see surface things—skin, wrinkles, dark circles—but others see beyond the surface. The depth of our vision, both figuratively and literally, determines what we see. That depth can shift depending on how we feel in any given moment. As I mentioned at the opening of this chapter, we can see both the physical markers of age, like wrinkles, and the wisdom that comes with them.

How deeply we allow ourselves to look makes all the difference. Are we looking only at what's on the surface, or are we able to see past that to what really matters? If we are looking at what needs to be "fixed," we reduce ourselves to a problem that needs to be solved. When that happens, we let the superficial define us without exploring what lies beneath. The secret to loving who we see in the mirror rests in how deeply we can connect with what we see. The source of our beauty lives in our connection to our true selves.

When we are in problem-solving mode, we are doing what we are good at: fixing things. And we are great problem-solvers, aren't we? We solve problems for family, friends, ourselves, and in the workplace. There is a sense of joy and purpose that comes from being helpful in this way. If you're anything like me, you take pride in your ability to find solutions. But here's the thing: The transactional nature of problem-solving can distract us from the deeper, transformative journey of aging. When there's no problem to fix, we often go looking for one—especially when we are unhappy with our reflection in the mirror.

If it's depth we seek, we won't find it in transactional thoughts about what we need to "fix."

HEAD-DRIVEN VERSUS HEART-DRIVEN

Have you heard of being "head-driven" versus "heart-driven"? These terms refer to how our problem-solving brains like to see the world. Neither approach is right or wrong—both are essential at different times. When we are head-driven, we leap into action, check off tasks, solve problems, and get things done. It's an efficient and practical mode of operation.

The heart-driven approach is different. The heart holds a deeper wisdom that's harder to define but incredibly powerful. It does not need checklists or plans. The heart offers us a view through a lens of compassion and insight that transcends surface-level concerns.

The heart is not here to fix things. It is here to guide us toward what matters most. Our heart can take in our reflection and see that there is nothing to "fix." There may be things we would like to enhance or adjust, but in a heart-driven approach, we see those things from a place of desire, not necessity. Being heart-driven means that we can access a source of strength and beauty that supports us as we age, allowing room for growth.

This is the key difference between Thoughtful Aging and anti-aging. Anti-aging focuses on problems to solve.

Thoughtful Aging recognizes that while challenges may come with aging, we can meet those changes with honor and grace.

Our hearts are gracious, too. They let us be distracted by surface thoughts without causing us pain. If you see your reflection in the mirror and feel a negative emotion, rest assured, that feeling is not coming from your heart. It's a distraction from your heart's true message. Our hearts are patient and kind. They wait until we are ready to listen, gently guiding us back to our true beauty. This is when transformation happens—when we stop and truly listen to the wisdom of our hearts.

A head-driven approach offers us a sense of safety. We know how to scan for problems and fix them, and that predictability can be comforting. Transactional living is predictable and consistent. But living through the heart takes courage. It requires honesty, curiosity, a grounded presence, and a desire to listen to the wisdom of the body.

I want to live in a world where women see their reflection and look past *what* they see to *whom* they see, the spark that ignites their glow. That spark can change from day to day. Some days, it might be recalling a kind gesture from the previous day that ignites your glow. It might be a loving word from a child or partner. It could even be a moment of appreciation for a beautiful blue sky. Each of us has our own unique glow, ignited by sparks throughout each day. It's what makes us who we are. It's the part of us that lights up when we step into confidence, show empathy to others, and practice kindness. Trust me, it is there. Personally speaking, it takes me a minute each morning to let the negative thoughts pass by and find a spark to ignite my glow. But I always feel so much better when I do. If you're having trouble feeling your glow, call up your best friend and ask her what she likes about you. Listen to what she says with an open heart. Your spark will ignite, and you'll feel your glow.

There are a million reasons why we might look or not look in a mirror. As you can see from the comments above, there are a lot of people who just don't because they don't want to see their reflections. They cannot accept what they see. I avoided my reflection for years. My insecurities and the shame I carried were the lens through which I saw myself. Carrying that burden was heavy enough; I didn't want to look at it in the mirror, too. When you are in this space, it helps to hold an appreciation for the woman still standing. There you are, beautiful you, still standing, still breathing, one day at a time. And if you can't bring yourself to see past your reflection to your glow just yet, close your eyes and focus on feeling it as a starting point.

Finding your glow will lead you to gratitude for your journey through time. After all, your glow is that essence of you that has been developed through trials and tribulations, successes and failures, good things, and challenging things. It is that earned wisdom every one of us possesses. That's what I want us to see when we look in a mirror: the essence that defines our beauty. How we choose to express it is uniquely up to us. Now go, sister, and play that soul song for everyone to hear!

DAILY PRACTICE: RECLAIMING BEAUTY IN YOUR REFLECTION

Below are daily practices I invite you to consider as ways to develop a compassionate relationship with your reflection and rediscover your unique beauty. These require intention; therefore, I have included a suggested time for each exercise.

1. Morning Mirror Affirmation (2 minutes)

Stand in front of the mirror each morning, and before you start examining your appearance, take a deep breath. Look into your eyes and focus on one thing you appreciate about yourself that is unrelated to your appearance. This could be your resilience, kindness, or creativity. Say out loud or in your mind: "I see you. I honor the person you are becoming, and I choose to treat you with kindness." Then gently smile at your reflection, even if it feels uncomfortable at first.

2. Gratitude for Your Body (3 minutes)

Take a moment to appreciate your body for what it does rather than how it looks. Think about three things your body does that you are grateful for. For example, *I am grateful for my legs that carry me, I appreciate my hands for letting me create,* or *I am thankful for my heart that beats steadily.* Place your hand over the area of your body you are grateful for and express silent or spoken gratitude.

3. Positive Reframing (2-3 minutes)

Each time you catch yourself being critical of your appearance throughout the day, stop and reframe the thought. For example, if you think *I look tired*, replace it with *I am doing my best, and it is okay to rest*. If you focus on a feature you don't like, shift your attention to something you find beautiful, like the color of your eyes or the curve of your smile. End each reframe with *I am enough, just as I am*.

4. Evening Reflection (2 minutes)

At the end of each day, return to the mirror for a quiet, nonjudgmental check-in. Look at yourself and reflect on one positive thing that happened during your day. It can be as simple as completing a task, having a kind conversation, or practicing self-care. Say: "I am proud of myself for (specific achievement) and I accept myself fully." The key to this practice is consistency. Over time, your relationship with your reflection will shift from critical observation to acceptance and appreciation. Be patient with yourself, knowing that this is a journey, not a quick fix.

Choose Who You See in the Mirror

Developing admirable character traits reflects resilience, inner strength, emotional intelligence, and a commitment to growth. These traits are admired in women who live authentically. Which do you value most?

Compassion — The ability to empathize with others and show kindness and understanding.

Integrity — Consistently aligning actions with values and being honest and trustworthy.

Resilience — The strength to recover from challenges and setbacks with grace.

Humility — A willingness to admit mistakes, learn from them, and stay grounded.

Courage — Facing fears, standing up for what is right, and taking risks when necessary.

Confidence — A sense of self-assurance without arrogance, rooted in one's abilities and worth.

Patience — The ability to stay calm and composed in difficult or stressful situations.

Gratitude — Recognizing and appreciating life's blessings, even in difficult times.

Wisdom — Applying knowledge and experience thoughtfully and making sound decisions.

Adaptability — The ability to embrace change and adjust to new circumstances.

Empowerment — Encouraging and supporting others while also valuing personal growth.

Perseverance — The commitment to keep striving toward goals, even in the face of adversity.

Grace — Handling success and failure with dignity, poise, and kindness.

Generosity — Willingness to give time, support, and resources to help others.

Self-Awareness — Understanding oneself, including one's strengths, weaknesses, and emotional triggers, and continuously working toward self-improvement.

Considering these character traits, complete the following sentences with the first thoughts that come to mind. There are no right or wrong answers. Remember, you can trust your intuition. You may want to get a notebook for your answers, as we'll be doing several exercises like this throughout the book.

I feel most aligned with my values when I _____

_____

_____

_____

A trait I aspire to strengthen within myself is_____

_____

_____

_____

In moments of challenge, I want to show more _____

_____

_____

_____

When I think about the person I want to become, I envision someone who _____

_____

_____

_____

I define success not by what I have, but by how I _____

_____

_____

_____

I believe my moral compass guides me toward decisions that reflect _____

_____

_____

_____

To live with greater integrity, I will strive to _____

_____

_____

_____

An inner quality I want to nurture moving forward is

_____

_____

_____

Chapter 5:

The Many Facets of Beauty

If we are used to focusing on or seeking out flaws, it can be hard to see beyond that initial scan when we look in the mirror. It can be hard to separate what our intuition and wisdom tells us from all the noise society, media, and the anti-aging industry throw at us. It can feel almost impossible to untangle the truth from what we've seen in hundreds of thousands of filtered social media selfies.

It's hard, but it's worth it. We can rediscover our beauty.

The best way to begin with this process (and it is a process; it is a journey of years) is to untangle those messages so we can better understand all the different aspects of women's beauty. We began this process all the way back in Chapter 1 and have been incorporating more ideas in every chapter since. But we haven't yet covered all the aspects of our beauty and how we present it. By unraveling some of the definitions and aspects of beauty, we will gain a lot of clarity about what kind of beauty we want for ourselves. We will also be less likely to be swayed by the types of messages that do not serve us.

Here are just a few of the aspects of beauty each woman holds.

BEAUTY AS CULTURE DEFINES IT

As discussed in previous chapters, for most of us, "culture" is Western culture. American culture. This is the lens that makes so many women feel invisible and less than. But it's everywhere, manipulating us and shaping how we see ourselves.

Honestly, not all of this is completely bad. Even if we don't meet this standard perfectly, we have probably been told we have "nice eyes," "good bone structure," or "great brows." In fact, we may well fit into this beauty standard more than we don't—we just tend to focus more on where we come up short. Almost everyone has some of these beauty attributes. Enhancing these attributes is the number one strategy professionals in medical cosmetics use to get maximum results with minimal effort or change.

These are the de facto, beauty culture-amplified American beauty standards:

- Clear, firm skin on the face

- Symmetry in face and body

- High cheekbones
- Full lips
- Large eyes
- Slimness
- Youth (which is completely subjective, of course, but generally construed as under thirty-five)
- Blonde hair
- Whiteness

Social media, TV, and advertising all promote these "standards." They also shape the several thousand beauty-related messages we receive each day—the same ones that bombard us with unrealistic images of people who started out with won-the-genetic-lottery looks and then were enhanced even more thanks to professional lighting and makeup.

These standards are also, clearly, based on "white" faces and bodies. It is impossible to talk about these beauty standards without acknowledging how white they are.

I want to approach this as humbly as possible because, as a white woman, I cannot know the experience of non-white women, whether in the realm of beauty culture or any other culture or aspect of culture. The gap in my understanding is obvious. I do see a commonality between myself, other white women, and women of color, though: We all know what it's like not to fit into the standard idea of beauty. No one meets the standard perfectly. I imagine even Barbie would probably have a few off days here and there, if she were real.

Falling short of beauty standards can cause deep pain, especially if you feel judgment from others or yourself for falling short. Even as I write that—"falling short"—I'm very aware that it carries implied blame for those who do not meet these standards.

Tristen Collins, a licensed professional counselor and life coach in Portland, Oregon, shares her story about not aligning with American beauty standards. I am including it here, with permission, in a spirit of perhaps shedding a little bit of understanding on even a sliver of what it can feel like to not fit into America's very white beauty standards:

> *We all have a complicated relationship with our bodies. When I was in elementary school, I already felt dissatisfied with the body God gave me. I'm Japanese American, and I really wanted to look like a Disney princess, like most girls my age.*
>
> *But in the '80s, they looked nothing like me. I wanted my hair to be blonde or brown, and my eyes to be bigger. Or at the very least, I wanted to blend in and not stand out. I looked very different than most of my classmates in my predominantly white school.*
>
> *My mind was often preoccupied with ideas of how to look and act less Asian. I didn't like my body, and I wanted to change it into something else. Kids*

would use their fingers to pull out the outside corners of their eyes as their attempt to look Asian. Their eyes became distorted, small slits, and they looked so ugly. I wondered if this was how they saw me.

I also remember a gross feeling in my stomach. I didn't have words for it then, but I do now. It was shame. A common response to feeling shame is to hide, but what if you have physical traits, like different eyes, different skin, or any physical difference that you can't keep hidden? You might develop contempt or dislike for your body. Contempt for our bodies can develop for those among us who have been emotionally, physically, and sexually mistreated or abused by others. You can be the most beautiful celebrity and still dislike your body.

As I got older, I started to feel less of a need to blend in, and I began to appreciate my physical differences. But now my struggle is with my aging body and trying to make peace with its limits. Everyone has experienced some variation of this, whether it's our face, our skin, our size, or the way our body moves.

No one is immune. We are all trained to be dissatisfied with our bodies. Our society bombards us with advertising and messaging, triggering us to feel dissatisfied with who we are, so we'll buy whatever they're selling.

We are sold the lie that if our body looks and functions a particular way, we will find happiness and love. We all have thoughts or experiences where we feel shame about our body. Find someone you trust to talk about your shame.[18]

Tristen's story beautifully illustrates the need to see past our own stories and into the heart of other people's lived experiences. Everyone has a story to share, defined—at least in part—by culture. Healing begins when we trade shame for compassion and honor the beauty that is uniquely ours.

BEAUTY AS DEFINED BY OUR FAMILY OR INNER CIRCLE

Our ideas about beauty are shaped by the smaller "culture" of our immediate family, our friends, and our communities.

Just be aware: A lot of the messaging we get about beauty is not from the media. The influence of our best friends, whatever the trends were in high school or in the social circles in which we traveled or travel—all those messages have taken root in us, too. If all your friends think wearing makeup is being self-indulgent, you are unlikely to wear much.

Of course, no one is as influential as our mothers (and mother figures). Hopefully, yours was and is a wonderful influence, but often our relationships with our mothers are more complicated.

Still, like it or not, when you start to examine how you view women's beauty and your own, you will discover a lot of your mother's ideas about beauty. Most likely, this is the person who taught you how to brush your hair and what was or was not okay to wear. This person also judged or supported you during critical transition times in your life. You watched her tend to her own beauty when you were a very little girl. You picked up a lot from her, consciously and unconsciously.

Barring the most egregious behavior, we do not and should not throw out everything our mothers taught us. That could be a terrible loss. Most of us reach a point in the story of our lives where we no longer identify with who we thought we were as the main character of our own story, and shift into identification with our mothers. We look in the mirror and see a resemblance to our aging mothers. We find ourselves saying things our mothers would say. It's a wakeup call, a reason to pause and examine our inner selves.

Those with a contentious mother/daughter relationship will do anything they can to avoid acting or looking like their mothers. Those with a healthy mother/daughter relationship will welcome those similarities. As a mother, I can tell you that every time my daughter mentions how happy she is that we look alike, I smile. When I think of my mother, I am grateful for her kind nature, patience, grace, and natural beauty.

BEAUTY BEYOND THE SURFACE

If we are going to define different types of outer beauty, it seems we ought to apply the same line of thinking to inner beauty as well. Our inner selves are easily as multi-dimensional as all the ways our outer beauty is perceived. I believe that it is our inner selves that are responsible for our true beauty, the type of beauty that radiates from within. We will talk much more about this in later chapters, but for now, I want to highlight different aspects of how our inner selves shape our outer appearance.

Our Personality

The way our inner beauty is talked about is often based on how loving or kind we are. As one of the women I interviewed for this book said, "My personality makes me feel beautiful." AARP's research on women's perceptions of beauty supports this. Most of the women in the study felt that their "beauty is more what kind of person they are, not what they look like." They placed their personalities, morals, values, and personality traits like kindness ahead of their personal appearance.[19]

Our inner beauty could also be described as our radiance or our spark. It is that inexplicable something some women possess—a confidence, connection, and warmth that draws people to them. This is the sort of beauty that many older women possess, especially those who honor their aging journey.

The character traits exercise you did (or didn't do, and that's okay) in the last chapter is a good way to begin enhancing this aspect of your beauty. The exploration of character and inner beauty is a lifelong practice, one that enhances not only how you feel about yourself, but also how others experience your presence. When you reflect on and deepen the character traits that make you unique, you also deepen your connection with yourself. When you nurture these traits, you naturally radiate beauty.

Our Self-Esteem

Our feelings about ourselves shape our inner beauty. Feeling fulfilled, connected, and lit-up about what's happening in our lives can give us a radiance that people recognize and want to connect with. Our self-esteem fuels our confidence. And despite being the tagline for a hair-coloring line, it is true that "Confidence is the new beautiful." In fact, 92% of women in a recent AARP study said that inner confidence is more important than outer beauty.[20]

Our Personal Style

How we feel about ourselves comes through in our grooming, how we dress, and our personal style. Many women who do not necessarily have the classic physical assets that American culture celebrates have learned how to dress and manage their appearance so well that we think of them as attractive anyway. Because they are.

Personalized, Unique Beauty

This is the type of beauty that ad campaigns are now trying to celebrate. It is an unconventional beauty—like the constellation of freckles on your best friend's face, or how some women may technically be overweight, but still look great. They are zaftig—"pleasantly plump or full-bodied."

These beauty characteristics do not fit the strict definition of magazine-style beauty. Some women just seem to wear them exceptionally well, or they seem somehow perfectly suited to their character. Individual women present this beauty in completely unique ways. And when this sort of beauty and her inner beauty are in sync, a woman may not fit into standard definitions of beauty at all and yet still be considered a great beauty.

Those are the most recognizable types of beauty. They are the lenses, contexts, ideas, and ideals through which we see our beauty and the beauty of others. These next aspects of beauty are more about our own experience of it—how we "use" beauty or what we get from it.

HOW WE USE OUR BEAUTY

As we saw in Chapter 1, most women say that attractiveness is a competitive advantage in life. Whether it is through gaining attention, receiving preferential treatment, or influencing others more easily, physical beauty often impacts how we are perceived and how we move through the world. While the ethics of leveraging beauty can be debated, the reality is that we live in a society where appearance holds considerable power. These are the ways in which women "use" their beauty, both consciously and unconsciously, and the effects they have on our interactions and experiences.

A WORD ABOUT "VANITY"

It's time to have a little discussion about the "V" word—vanity. Merriam-Webster defines vanity as:

1 : *inflated pride in oneself or one's appearance :*
CONCEIT

2 : *something that is vain, empty, or valueless*[21]

Examining the official definition of vanity is helpful because it is a word that is often misused or misunderstood. Have you ever stopped to consider that there is more than one way to look at vanity? We have been conditioned to think of vanity in terms of good or bad, right or wrong. But when we view vanity this way, it turns self-care into a moral dilemma, oftentimes leaving us feeling guilty for looking after our appearance.

The truth is that each of us experiences vanity differently. For me, it is tied to the right-and-wrong teachings of religious principles. For someone else, the word might remind them of how they were teased by a sibling or parent for looking at themselves in the mirror. And for others, it may hold no meaning at all. It is deeply personal and influenced by our unique life experiences, so it is unlikely that we can all agree on a single definition.

I propose that from this point forward, you allow yourself the freedom to redefine vanity on your own terms. Does it have to be negative? Could it be positive? Personally, I believe self-care is often misinterpreted as vanity. If someone wants to call me vain for taking care of myself in a way that feels true to me, I will wear that label with pride. Their definition of vanity is theirs to hold, not mine to carry. My responsibility is to define it for myself and stand confidently in that definition.

As a society, we have understandably turned vanity into a word that incites moral judgment—again, just look at the official definition. But I want to make it clear: There is no place for judgments of right or wrong in this conversation about beauty. Vanity is not inherently right or wrong; it is a concept shaped for each of us by our personal experiences and beliefs. It is time we let go of imposing those personal beliefs on others and move beyond moral labels when it comes to self-care.

Using Our Beauty to Get Attention

Like it or not, everyone knows that if you are beautiful or unusually attractive, you can get away with more. You get more attention. You can more easily sway people to do what you want. Women know that how we look powerfully shapes how we are treated. Whether it is "right" or "wrong" for the world to be this way and whether it is "right" or "wrong" for a woman to leverage this for her benefit are separate questions. The reality is we live in a superficial world. Beautiful women wield a certain kind of power.

This came to my awareness in high school, when I found it easy to get extensions on assignment deadlines or arrive late to class with no penalty. The subtle privileges that came with my appearance continued throughout my life—free coffee from baristas, extra help from men at the hardware store or priority service at the auto repair shop, compliments that often blurred the line between admiration and favoritism. I wasn't oblivious to what was happening, but I didn't question it either. Comments such as "You're too pretty to worry about that," meant as flattery, left me feeling conflicted. On one hand, the ease that came with my looks made life smoother in small but significant ways. On the other hand, I wondered if people saw me for who I truly was or simply for how I looked. When people make assumptions about us based on appearance, it leaves little room for them to see us beyond that. To feel truly seen is to be appreciated for who we are inside, too; but if we are consistently put in a box based on how we look, it becomes difficult to break free, especially if everyone is rewarding and complimenting us for staying in it.

I also questioned whether it was ethical to accept these advantages. That's when I began to get curious about *why* it was happening. Part of me felt that I should take a stand against the superficial standards that placed such weight on appearance. But another part of me recognized that learning to navigate these superficial standards required a balance between awareness and self-acceptance.

People Make Assumptions Based on How We Look

People assume—incorrectly or not—that beautiful people are smarter, more capable, and even somehow morally better than people who are less attractive. Anyone thinking about it carefully will see that this assumption is ridiculous, but it is one almost all of us make.

I have experienced this bias firsthand in job interviews. On three different occasions, I was offered the job immediately after the interview. Each time, I wondered, "Is this offer because of my qualifications or because of how I look?" The question remains unanswered, but it has stayed with me over the years. How much of my privilege was due to assumptions others made about me based on my appearance?

Despite the attention, such interactions left me feeling invisible. It took me years to figure out how to bridge the gap between how people saw me and who I truly was. Misunderstandings often arose when others filled that gap with their own assumptions about me, which were rarely positive. I learned that in my quiet confidence, I was perceived as unapproachable and intimidating. I realized that I had to take the lead in creating connection—offering a smile, initiating a conversation, or giving a compliment to invite others into a moment of genuine interaction. This growth was uncomfortable for me at first but has been delightfully rewarding ever since.

Several years ago, I was invited to attend an event at my son's workplace, a call center for a national cellular service provider. He asked me to arrive early so he could show me around and introduce me to the teams he was leading. Since it was also a workday for me, I arrived in my usual silk top, pencil skirt, and four-inch heels. If you haven't been in a call center before, I can tell you that the dress code is very casual. Most wear jeans and sweatshirts and don't dress to impress anyone. As my son walked me around, I noticed that people seemed very uncomfortable around me, though I was smiling, greeting people, and being as friendly as the limited time would allow. He called me after I left to tell me that everyone was convinced I was from "corporate" and had "come down from the top" to take a tour of the call center. My appearance, and their preconceived idea of who I was because of how I was dressed, overshadowed their ability to connect with me as their highly respected team leader's mother. My son's colleagues could not see—or even believe—who I was due to the assumptions they made about me because of how I looked. They were, in a sense, unable to see the real me.

Using Our Beauty to Gain Approval

Because appearances are so powerful, we can and do adjust our looks to please others—like our partner or boyfriend, or someone we would like to be our partner or boyfriend. But we can also adjust our looks to please our families. Everyone knows what it feels like to walk into a room and have our mother, father, or some other family member say, "Oh, don't you look nice" or give us a smile of approval.

I have definitely adjusted my appearance to please people, but not in a way that feels like I am losing myself—for me, it has been more of a choice. When I was younger, I spent hours styling my hair or choosing the right outfit so that I could stand out just enough to be noticed. Being raised in a conservative Christian household, there were very strict standards for what was allowed for my sisters and me. All skirts had to hit below the knee, we were allowed to wear jeans only once a week, and we had to keep our shoulders covered when we were out in public. Pantyhose and nail polish were not allowed until we turned sixteen. Piercings of any kind were forbidden. These standards did not allow me to express myself in a way that was genuine and authentic to me, but following them did garner compliments from my mother, who holds those standards to this day. So much so that when my twelve-year-old granddaughter arrived at a Christmas dinner wearing a holiday outfit that exposed her shoulders, my mother's way of offering her guidance was to shame her into feeling underdressed. While her intentions are good, she continues to hold a perspective based on judgment and fear of "what men might do" to an "underdressed" woman. Fortunately, my granddaughter is on a path to breaking this shame cycle and can stand confidently in her own choices. She uses these opportunities to determine her own set of values rather than allow them to be defined for her by others.

It's nice to get approval and compliments from family, but it's not necessary. And there is a balance we reach as we grow more confident; we can appreciate the compliments without needing them to validate who we are. When I dress up for an event or style my hair in a certain way, it is because I like the way it makes me feel. If it also happens to please the people around me, that's just a bonus.

Using Our Beauty to Make a Positive Impression

We adjust our beauty for work and social events. We use our looks, clothes, and makeup as a way to communicate with others. The way we show up sends a message—whether it is "dressing for the job we want" at work or showing up in rumpled clothing with our hair unwashed. We may not always realize it, but how we present ourselves communicates volumes.

I met Danielle Van Auken, founder of Organic Bronze Bar, many years ago. At that time, she was just forming what is now a national franchise of organic airbrush tanning salons. Her first—and, at the time, only—salon was located next door to a medical aesthetics clinic I had opened in downtown Portland. I saw her often and noticed that she was always dressed nicely in skirts or jeans, beautiful tops, heels, and appropriate makeup. This lady could even make a baseball cap look stylish. In contrast, I showed up to work in scrubs, with plain hair and minimal makeup. We both owned businesses and were representing them in opposite ways. I asked her one day why she always looked so well put-together and beautiful. She replied, "I never know who I am going to meet on any given day. I might meet someone who can help me grow my business—or someone who knows someone who can help. You just never know whose path will cross yours, and first impressions matter." Danielle showed up each day, ready for whatever came her way, with a mindset of possibility. In contrast, I showed up each day just waiting for whatever came my way without even a thought about what that might be.

Using Our Beauty
to Feel Good About Ourselves

We know when we're wearing clothing that makes us look exceptionally good. We can see when people notice, when they flash a smile of appreciation and admiration. I took my conversation with Danielle to heart and began putting thought and effort into presenting myself in a way that I felt was more aligned with what I wanted for my business. I began wearing heels daily (which I still love) and outfits that reflect what beauty means to me. What I noticed almost immediately was that, as I started to present myself with intention, I also began to see possibility. My mindset shifted from waiting for opportunities to come along, hoping things would work out, to seeking opportunities to help myself and others.

There is a reason so many women enjoy dressing up and going out. It feels good to look good. Looking good gives us pleasure and boosts our confidence. This is—or should be—the best reason to enhance our looks. Because it feels good. It makes us happy. It's *fun*. And in this sense, our feelings are influenced by how we know we look.

> **Feeling attractive makes me happier and more outgoing overall!**
>
> **—Survey respondent**

However, we must be wary of allowing our desire to appear beautiful to overshadow the fact that we *are* beautiful. Makeup is simply a way to access different versions of ourselves, a form of social currency that can make it easier to navigate a world that often prioritizes appearance. But here's the real question: Are you comfortable in your own beauty, with or without makeup?

I challenge you to embrace and understand both worlds—the one where makeup helps you express a part of yourself and the one where your natural beauty stands on its own. Each of these worlds offers a unique experience of self-discovery. Learning to navigate both can reveal layers of confidence and self-acceptance you might not have known were there. By exploring both sides, you may unlock parts of yourself that have been quietly waiting for your attention, regardless of whether you're wearing makeup or not.

My grandmother connected to her beauty without using makeup. I'm not sure she even owned a lipstick. She raised twelve children on an eighty-acre farm in rural Minnesota, losing one to leukemia and saving one from polio. She grew her own food, washed clothes with water from a well, did all her cooking and baking on a wood stove, and had no indoor bathroom. Her day began before sunrise. She stood tall, moved quickly, and always wore an apron.

The only beauty routine I observed happened in the evenings, when her work was done. After changing into her nightclothes, she removed the pins holding up her bun and let her long silver hair fall. It was then, with her bristled brush in hand, that she cared for herself with intention. I watched as her breath went from shallow to deep. In those moments, she was able to close her eyes and return to her essence despite any weight of responsibility she may have felt.

My grandmother embodied a noticeable grace and elegance in the way she carried herself, spoke with kindness, and cared for us. These qualities were not based solely on beauty or appearance, although she was beautiful. She had very few, if any, store-bought clothes; she made her own, choosing patterns and fabrics that complemented her coloring, body type, and style. I'm certain she felt quite confident in her appearance when a neighbor stopped by for an unexpected visit. Her embodiment of beauty came from who she chose to be as a mother, wife, friend, sister, and daughter. These choices and what she believed about herself formed her identity, which was no doubt influenced by her expression of beauty.

HOW BEAUTY INFLUENCES OUR IDENTITY

Those are the most common interpretations and experiences of women's beauty. You may see yourself in one or all of them. Or you may remember when one type or experience of beauty seemed so easy and effortless, while now it feels like those days are past.

> **So much emphasis is placed on looks from the time you are a young lady. It becomes a part of your identity and then it just fades away. It's just true that the world treats you better when you look a certain way. Can we start an "aging positivity" movement?**
>
> **—Survey respondent**

If one of those experiences or aspects of beauty is not as active in your life anymore, that is okay. Our beauty changes. How we see and experience beauty changes. It should; as our experiences deepen, our perspectives change. We evolve.

We've all experienced a point when we felt pulled toward or pushed away from our own interpretation of beauty. Think back to your younger years, when you were a girl. Did you receive a makeup kit? Can you remember what that was like? Did you see endless artistic possibilities, or were you terrified of trying and failing? Or maybe you weren't sure why anyone would ever want to put that stuff on their face. What did beauty mean to you with that makeup kit in your hands? Were you excited to see how you could change your look, or did it feel daunting?

Maybe you had a more memorable experience painting your nails. Did your nine-year-old self pretend you were a princess when your best friend painted your nails? Or were you focused on that little bit brushed onto your cuticle? Did your parents encourage you or shame you? Did you experience shame and ridicule when your early fashion choices ended up as fashion faux pas, or did someone quietly pull you aside to suggest just a tiny change that fixed everything? I was all in on being The Possibilities Princess—but I was probably more accurately a walking fashion faux pas.

Our early encounters with beauty shape our viewpoint of what beauty means to us. Our experience as girls lays the template for our experience as women. Whether we realize it or not, our early experiences influence how we embrace and define ourselves at a fundamental level.

My first awareness of the power of beauty was watching my mother prepare for my father's arrival home from work each day. Her routine began around our nap time. I often awoke from a nap to see her clothes changed and rollers in her hair. Shortly before he came home, she would stop everything, take out the rollers, dab a bit of Avon rose-scented perfume on her neck and wrists, and apply pink lipstick. She did all this while caring for four young children, preparing dinner, and making sure the house was in some semblance of order before he walked through the door.

It wasn't the act of fixing her hair or putting on lipstick that intrigued me. It was how she changed when she did. She went from what seemed like a busy, overworked mother to a confident woman in just a few simple steps. She stood taller, she spoke louder, and she smiled. It was in these moments that I realized: Beauty is defined by how we feel, not how we look. There was no magic in her lipstick; it was simply a tool she used to access a different version of herself.

It wasn't until I reflected on these memories as an adult that I truly understood what I had witnessed. The lipstick and perfume my mother used allowed her to access a version of herself that felt more expressive and aligned with the beauty she carried inside. My awareness as a child was an early glimpse into this shift, but it took years for me to fully comprehend the deeper change I saw in her—her ability to draw from her inner beauty, according to her own standard and even amidst the chaos of daily life. This realization deepened my belief that beauty is rooted not in how we look, but in how we feel.

Throughout my life, I have asked myself: *If I view makeup as a social currency (and I do), can I use it to increase my confidence in new ways? What parts of myself remain undiscovered because I'm afraid to try something new? And what is it that I am afraid of?* Then I remember one of my favorite transformative tools: red lipstick.

ADVENTURE AND RED LIPSTICK

I have met very few women who are brave enough to wear a bold red lipstick. When I taught women how to apply makeup, I often asked how they felt about red lipstick. Probably nine out of ten women said something like, "Oh, me? I could never do that. I would never wear red lipstick." Like there's something dangerous about red lipstick! When I asked them why not, the most common answer was, "Well, that's just not me"—even though red lipstick was something they had never tried.

I held this belief myself until May of 2020. The world was on lockdown, and there I was, homebound and desperate for adventure of any sort. I had hit my quarantine wall. I felt the last fragments of hope fly off into the sunset as I sat in a hot bath with a bottle of prosecco and a carton of orange juice, eating Nutella by the spoonful while contemplating smoking a random cigarette I had found on the mantel downstairs. As I stared out the window, listening to the rain fall, I decided that I would have to create my own adventure. I found that adventure in my makeup drawer in the form of red lipstick. I had collected several tubes over the years, so I pulled them all out. It was time.

The first color wasn't right. It was an orange-red that didn't match my skin tone. The second, a brownish-red, was okay but didn't impress me. It was the third, a blue-red, that captivated me. I felt a new sense of confidence blossoming when I put it on. Alongside that confidence was a feeling of uncertainty. *Can I really pull this off? What will I wear it with? What will other people say? How will I ever feel comfortable with this color on my lips? I'm not one to seek attention, and red lipstick is all but a neon sign asking to be noticed.*

I decided to create a routine around it. It just so happened that my field needed mowing. I made my way to the tractor, climbed on, and mowed the field with my red lipstick leading the way. From that point on, every time I mowed the field, I wore red lipstick. No longer something I felt limited by or afraid of, it became something I looked forward to. I still use it to motivate me to do things I don't really want to do, like dishes or laundry. Somehow, wearing red lipstick turns menial tasks into pleasurable events. Now I wear it confidently on any day, at any time, and I love how it makes me feel.

Adventure comes in all shapes and sizes. No matter your adventure of choice, how about dressing it up with a pretty red lipstick?

EXERCISE: DEFINE YOUR BEAUTY

What does beauty mean to you? Contemplate your answers to the following questions in the days ahead. Give yourself time and return to this as answers come to you. Write down your answers in a journal, notebook, or on the following page.

What do you think makes women beautiful? _____

_____

_____

_____

_____

_____

What can you do to embody or embrace the traits that you think make women beautiful?_____

_____

_____

_____

_____

_____

What are your best physical features? _____

_____

_____

_____

_____

_____

_____

What can you do to appreciate your best features during the upcoming week? _____

_____

_____

_____

_____

_____

_____

HOW BEAUTY INFLUENCES ACCEPTANCE

While we're told it's shallow or undesirable to be influenced by the opinions of others, let's be real: we are. We are absolutely sensitive to the feedback from people around us. We'd be sociopaths if we weren't.

At one point in my life, my friends had a complex—and not entirely good—influence on me. Their discussions about anti-aging products, cosmetic procedures, diets, and fashion trends were superficial, but their focus on these things was also a reflection of deeper insecurities and societal pressures. I felt caught up in this and found myself making choices with my appearance that were heavily influenced by the collective mindset of my friends. For example, when a close friend decided to undergo a cosmetic procedure, I felt a subtle pressure to consider a similar option even though it wasn't what

I wanted. The choices my friends made created a ripple effect, subtly shaping my decisions as I navigated my own feelings about aging and beauty. The fear of being left behind, of not keeping up with the group's standards, caused me to consider choices that aligned more with my friends' expectations than my own.

We are influenced by how others see us. How others view us matters, whether we're at work, on a date, or even out running errands. How we are treated shapes our identity. The three aspects of beauty—how the world defines beauty, how we define beauty, and how we present our beauty—overlap and inform each other.

Every woman knows this because every woman has experienced it. Depending on who we are and what phase of life we're in, we may put almost no effort into how we look or an enormous amount of effort into how we look. The key is to make our choice with awareness and confidence.

> **The realization that my looks are a big part of my identity just kind of slapped me in the face. I went from turning heads when I walked into a room to being the old lady in the corner. I had never thought of my appearance as being part of who I am.**
>
> **—Survey respondent**

Many of the beauty choices we make are about fitting in. But do we really need to fit in? Sure, conformity often facilitates acceptance and reduces conflict. As I mentioned in Chapter 3, we are social beings who seek belonging and validation from our friends and family. Conforming can make it easier to build relationships and find common ground with others, both of which are necessary for acceptance. However, true acceptance ideally goes beyond superficial conformity and embraces individuality. What if you could bypass the desire for acceptance? What would it feel like to be the person who offers acceptance rather than depends upon it? How would that change your social experiences? Your anxiety level?

Enter self-confidence. You may not think it has anything to do with acceptance, but it does. Confidence stems from accepting ourselves fully, to the point where we become naturally comfortable in our own skin and less reliant on external validation. It also embodies other key aspects of Thoughtful Aging, such as authenticity, resilience, and a positive mindset. Confident people radiate acceptance of themselves and others from within, enabling them to navigate life with grace.

My confidence blossomed when I began to differentiate between the choices that genuinely reflected my own values and desires and those that were simply echoes of the collective mindset of my friends and family. It wasn't about abandoning my friendships or my family, but about redefining the terms of my life in a way that allowed me to be authentic, even if that meant redefining how I related to others.

Chapter 6:

Relationships: Staying Connected as We Stay True to Ourselves

Women with strong friendships tend to live longer and healthier lives. By turning to friendships during stressful times, we are not only protecting ourselves emotionally, but also physically. A 2006 UCLA study led by Dr. Shelley E. Taylor suggests that women's friendships reduce stress through "tend and befriend" responses. When we face high-stress situations, we are more likely to nurture and care for ourselves and others (tend) and seek social support from others, particularly friends, as a coping mechanism (befriend). One of the key findings of this research is the role of oxytocin, a "feel-good" hormone that is present in these social bonding and nurturing experiences.[22] Oxytocin helps counteract the effects of stress by inducing feelings of calm, relaxation, and trust. When women turn to friends during times of stress, oxytocin levels rise, which reduces the production of cortisol (the stress hormone). In essence, friendships that nurture feelings of comfort and connection become a natural stress-relief mechanism. Friendships provide a buffer against life's inevitable stressors—a safety net that can keep us engaged rather than isolated.

My close friends have supported me through the many challenges I have faced, whether the anxieties of aging, the emotional complexities of family life, or the professional setbacks that sometimes shook my confidence. They have offered me more than surface-level comfort, providing a safe space where I could express my fears, insecurities, and doubts without judgment and helping me to be vulnerable in ways I rarely allowed myself to be elsewhere. Their encouragement has had a profound impact on my ability to reconnect with myself.

Relationships and beauty are intrinsically linked because how we relate to others often mirrors and influences how we view ourselves. And so, as we develop a deeper sense of internal beauty, we are better equipped to build relationships that honor who we truly are. For example, if others view us as insecure, they may pull away. If they see us as confident, they may feel safe in our presence. If we project inner peace, they may find it easier to be content in quiet moments.

My friends see qualities in me that I have sometimes struggled to see in myself. They support my resilience, kindness, and intelligence. And their belief in me gives me the courage to embrace these aspects of my identity.

MEET YOUR MIRROR NEURONS

Have you ever felt "in sync" with another person? Our brain's ability to reflect other people's emotions and behaviors is more than a metaphor.

Marco Iacoboni, a leading neuroscientist at UCLA, discusses what it means to create a bridge between self and others in his book *Mirroring People: The New Science of How We Connect.* In it, he discusses how mirror neurons, a small circuit of cells in the cerebral cortex, are activated both when we do things and when we observe others doing things.

The social signals we make through gestures, facial expressions, and body postures are a channel of communication. Mirror neurons allow us to understand other people by giving us an experience of what they are feeling and doing. When I see you smile, my mirror neurons for smiling fire up, initiating a cascade of neural activity that evokes the feeling we typically associate with a smile. I don't need to interpret what you are feeling because I am experiencing what you are feeling. In the same way, if you are anxious, talking really fast, and unable to focus on one thing, I may begin to experience anxiety, take shallow breaths, and impulsively take a step back because my mirror neurons are responding to what you are experiencing. We are having, in a sense, a shared experience; it is not as pleasant a shared experience as smiling, though, so I may feel the urge to step back.[23]

Mirror neurons also play a role in helping us deepen our connection to our inner beauty, as they allow us to experience empathy and compassion when we observe the actions and emotions of others. Experiencing empathy and compassion is an activation of our inner beauty, so when our mirror neurons are activated, our beauty resonates with that of others. When we see someone acting with integrity, kindness, or courage, our mirror neurons can evoke a similar response within us. This opens a door to self-reflection, where we recognize and appreciate our own moments of authenticity and the beauty that lies in being true to ourselves.

Through the process of mirroring others, we have the opportunity to reflect on our own behaviors and values. Recognizing traits in others and then feeling them within ourselves can make us more aware of our inner beauty, especially if we are around positive people who are connected to their own beauty. These compassionate responses to the feelings of others allow us to connect deeply with them.

Without an understanding of the role mirror neurons play in our relationships, we are limited in how we connect with others. We are more likely to misinterpret, react defensively, or struggle to build the trust and intimacy essential for healthy relationships. A lack of understanding about mirror neurons can also make us vulnerable to picking up other people's negative behaviors and feelings. Just as we can mirror positive feelings, we can mirror negative ones. Unconsciously mirroring negative behaviors can perpetuate cycles of misunderstanding and conflict between family members, friends, and intimate partners. But once we recognize the influence of mirror neurons, we are empowered to approach interactions with more empathy, understanding, and an ability to break free from unhealthy or harmful patterns.

Here is the simplest way to understand it: Emotions can be contagious. If you are particularly expressive or have strong emotional reactions, your partner's mirror neurons may cause them to pick up on and reflect your emotions. This can lead to a feedback loop where emotions—positive or negative—are amplified between you both.

Once you understand what's happening, you can manage your emotional responses more effectively. You might want to ask for a moment to step away or use breathwork to feel present again. Your partner will likely pick up on the resulting shift in you and stretch to meet you where you are. If they choose to remain dysregulated, try relating to them from a place of compassion. I promise you that no one wakes up in the morning and says to themselves, "Today I'm going to struggle. Today I want to feel bad." We all have challenging days. As women, we have a deep capacity to resolve conflict peacefully and bring harmony back to our relationships.

YOUR STORY MATTERS

When I first began the journey of rebuilding my life after my second marriage ended, I celebrated each new awareness with gratitude for where I had been and the limitless possibilities which lay before me. I also felt unsteady at times, questioning whether this newfound depth of connection was real. Why hadn't anyone taught me this? Why weren't any of my girlfriends talking about these things? Could it be that they, too, were on hidden journeys, in search of their true selves and seeking growth in new ways?

There were friends I had known since high school, some from my twenties and beyond, and even more I had met through the workplace to whom I had never truly opened up beyond seeking guidance for a specific problem or two. I was much more comfortable being the "good listener" and offering advice when needed. A dear friend said to me one day, "You never say anything about yourself. Tell me something about you." I honestly didn't know how to respond. "What do you mean?" I asked. A brief conversation revealed the truth: I was living a solitary life, hidden behind uncertainty and fear, and happy to play the conversational wallflower to others' life experiences. The cost of my lifelong practice of letting others see only a very limited version of myself was clear. Even though I had a very full life, I felt invisible and alone.

This compassionate lady artfully and carefully extracted my life story. And oh boy, did I have a lot to say. I found myself standing at my kitchen sink with tears streaming down my face, listening to the words coming out of my mouth and objectively wondering how they had become my life story. A mixture of emotions overwhelmed me: I felt embarrassed by the decisions I'd made, confused about what to do next, honored that my friend held my heart so tenderly, and grateful to be relieved of this burden of silence.

For the first time, I allowed myself to be seen, faults and all. And not just by her, but by me. Now don't get me wrong: My husband at the time knew my story, my children knew my story, and my family of origin knew my story. But there is something sacred about the vulnerability women share. We have the ability to offer healing to each other at a level which cannot be replicated. Do you know that about yourself? You have the capacity to heal, to fill another's heart with compassion. Ladies, we are amazing!

I spent the rest of that afternoon wondering why I was so uncomfortable talking about myself. I had a few close friends, many good friends, and innumerable acquaintances. Any number of them would gladly have listened to me talk about anything. They often came to me for advice, yet I never shared about myself, even when asked. The answer to why became clear: because that would make my story real. My perception of my life was much different from the life I found myself describing to my friend that day. The person I told her about had lived through much more than I ever thought I would tolerate. If I had been vulnerable enough to share the reality of my life along the way, it's likely I would have left my marriage years before I did. I would have made different parenting decisions, different financial decisions, and possibly different career decisions. But because I had chosen a solitary approach to life, I did not have the benefit of reflecting with others who might have seen what I did not.

I'd always felt I had been accountable for my life choices, but clearly, I had not. Superficially, yes. Internally, I wasn't so sure. That afternoon, I made a commitment to myself to pursue vulnerability. Doing so would require discernment. Not everyone deserved to hear my story. I knew who my close friends were and felt confident that they would welcome the expansion of our friendships through transparency and vulnerability. I took baby steps into this new territory. I shared little bits at a time until I became comfortable owning my story. It was both cathartic and liberating.

As I said in Chapter 3, I was balancing many new-found truths against what I had thought others expected of me. I was being more honest about what I truly believed, even if that did not match what some people in my life believed. My desire to live authentically kept me going, even through uncomfortable conversations and misunderstandings. Change is uncomfortable, to be sure. But at a certain point, resisting change is even more uncomfortable.

THE FOUR TYPES OF CONNECTION

The healing I experienced through deepening my friend-ships got me curious about why we live such lonely lives. Was loneliness just part of being human?

Dr. Curt Thompson, a psychiatrist, speaker, and author, says we are all born into the world looking for someone looking for us. And we remain in this mode of searching for the rest of our lives.[24]

Did you know that the percentage of Americans who say they have no close friends quadrupled between 1990 and 2020? According to a study by the Roots of Loneliness Project, 58% of Americans say that no one knows them well and 36% report that they feel lonely frequently or almost all of the time. That number goes up to 51% for young mothers and 61% for young adults.[25] And from a health standpoint, loneliness is worse for your health than smoking fifteen cigarettes a day.

The digital age has traded the illusion of connectivity for the reality of community. Dr. Robin Dunbar famously coined what sociologists refer to as "The law of 150." This law states that human beings cannot be in relationship with more than 150 people at a time. In our hyperconnected digital age, we have an illusion of connectivity, but it's not community. Dr. Dunbar's explanation of these friend groups, outlined below, helped me greatly.

Inner Circle

These are your intimate friends, the one to five people, maximum, who deeply know and love you as you are. These are the people to whom you bare your soul: your best friend, spouse, partner, mentor, sister, brother, mom, dad, grandparent, etc.

Friends

This group is fifteen people max. You do life with these people: you vacation together, shop together, and dine together. They help you move and show up in a crisis.

Acquaintances

This group could comprise up to 150 people. You draw on these people for networking. These are people you know through other people or have met in passing.

Tribe

You don't know these people personally, but you identify with them through church, activity groups, and/or political groups.[26]

Dr. Dunbar says that healthy people have relationships across all four circles, but our deepest growth, healing, and change happen within the two smallest circles. We connect through our weaknesses, not just our strengths.

All the lines that divide us—race, gender, politics, religion, etc.—can be erased to form us into communities of women who can lift each other up with humility and grace. But this does not happen by accident. Ladies, we must choose this. It is within this space that we can grow together. To create this community of support and growth, let's start with intentional action. Reach out to a friend, initiate a conversation, or join a group where women uplift one another. Commit to building these connections and together, let's form a network that thrives on empathy, understanding, and shared strength.

> **I need to choose some new friends who aren't just focused on their looks but are willing to do nice things for others. I just met two new friends this year. Gathering my crew for the final chapter.**
>
> **—Survey respondent**

PRACTICE RECEIVING COMPLIMENTS

Compliments are a bid for connection. One of the greatest gifts we can receive from all four friend groups and strangers alike is the gift of a compliment. Have you ever paid another woman a compliment only for her to dismiss it? I see this in the clinic nearly every day. We may not realize it, but we put up blocks. When someone compliments our outfit, we reply with a comment about our weight. When we're offered a compliment on our hair, we reply with, "Thanks, but I wish it wasn't so frizzy." Someone compliments us on our makeup, or a new lipstick we're wearing, and we justify our desire to try something new, as if we owe anyone an explanation.

When you deflect a compliment with a self-deprecating comment, you reject the giver's sincere attempt to connect. In a subtle way, you dismiss or even invalidate the compliment. By doing this, you create a void in that moment where beauty and connection could have flourished. Offers of connection and appreciation, when received with gratitude and grace, are micro-bonding experiences that can fuel your spark and bring beauty to your day.

Neurobiologists tell us that when people feel "felt" in conversation—seen, heard, and deeply listened to in a compassionate and intentional way—it is indistinguishable from feeling loved. This is also, of course, another opportunity for our mirror neurons to activate.

In his book *How to Know a Person*, David Brooks writes that "There's one skill that lies at the heart of any healthy person, family, school, community, organization or society—the ability to see someone else deeply and make them feel seen. To accurately know another person and let them feel valued, heard and understood. This is at the heart of being a good person."[27]

But here's the catch, scary as it may seem: You must want to be seen. Depth, vulnerability, and a commitment to transformation are requirements for growth. Fostering relationships that honor these values demands discipline, intentionality, and self-sacrifice. There is no way to fully heal past pain and trauma without being vulnerable and transparent in friendship with others. I have been on both sides of this fence and can tell you, beauty flourishes within connection.

RELATIONSHIP DYNAMICS: FOUR WAYS WE RELATE TO OTHERS

And yet, connection isn't always straightforward. The dynamics of our relationships, especially as we age, become increasingly complex. The older we get, the more we crave independence and authenticity. However, anyone with an aging parent will tell you the difficulties they face when help is required but not wanted.

What do we do when a loved one or dear friend refuses to accept desperately needed help? I know how frustrating that can be. I have aging parents, too. Understanding dependence, independence, interdependence, and codependence can help us cultivate healthier, more fulfilling relationships based on mutual respect and support. It also gives us the power to choose how we relate to others. It creates the opportunity to change what we don't like.

These dynamics play a role in our relationships with friends, family, and, of course, intimate partners and spouses. As we briefly define each concept, a certain person (or people) may pop into your mind. What I would like you to do as we move through this section is contemplate *your* role in each of those relationships. Recognize that any feeling of defensiveness or frustration is an invitation for you to explore a deeper part of yourself. Get curious and approach these feelings without blame or judgment.

Dependence

Dependence occurs when one person relies heavily on the other for emotional, financial, or personal support. This often leads to imbalances in the relationship and makes one or both people feel insecure. Adult children often fall into this category, as do low-functioning parents.

Codependence

Codependence, which we've all heard so much about, is characterized by an unhealthy reliance on each other's approval or well-being. This often leads to one person sacrificing their own needs and boundaries for the sake of the relationship, which in turn leads to resentment, exhaustion, and confusion. I was in my early twenties when I first read Melody Beattie's revolutionary book *Codependent No More*.[28] If you haven't read it, I highly recommend it. Codependence is often accompanied by passive-aggressive behavior. You know... that person whose smile tells you they are happy but whose body language says they would like to stab you with a fork.

Interdependence

Interdependence is a more balanced approach. Here, people support each other's needs and growth while maintaining their individual identities. This allows them to foster a mutually beneficial and respectful connection. This is a beautiful space in which to operate.

Independence

Independence involves each person maintaining their own interests, goals, and sense of self. This can be healthy, but if it is taken too far, it can also lead to emotional distance. I was fiercely attached to my independence as a young adult. I believed that I had to take care of myself on my own and I couldn't trust anyone. I was skeptical of any new ideas or information, which felt like a threat to my independence (read: safety).

The sweet spot for human interactions is an intentional flow between independence and interdependence. This is true for all healthy adult relationships, whether in marriages or partnerships, when adult children are caring for aging parents, or in business.

BOUNDARIES ARE NOT BARRIERS

Before we proceed, I want to acknowledge that the topic of boundaries may be activating (triggering) for some readers, especially those who have had this word used against them as a weapon of manipulation and control. If this is true for you, I encourage you to do your best to keep an open mind and mentally replace the word "boundaries" with "guidelines."

Boundaries are often misunderstood because they are perceived as barriers or signs of separation rather than tools for healthy relationships. Many people equate boundaries with rejection or control and fear that setting them will cause conflict or distance. Additionally, cultural and societal norms for women often promote the idea of self-sacrifice and putting others' needs first, which can make personal boundaries seem selfish or unnecessary.

Boundaries can also be misunderstood because they are deeply personal. They can vary widely from one person to another, leading to confusion about what constitutes a reasonable or fair limit for behavior. One person's boundary can be another person's disappointment.

Misunderstandings can also arise when boundaries are not communicated clearly or if they are enforced inconsistently, causing others to misinterpret them as arbitrary or rigid. Recognizing that boundaries are essential for maintaining balance, respect, and emotional well-being can help shift this perception and encourage healthier interactions and relationships. My work with Diane Ulicsni, an EMDR practitioner and life coach, taught me that the definition of a healthy boundary is not me telling you what I need you to do; it is me telling you what I will do under what conditions.[29] Let's explore healthy boundaries within a common dynamic between adult children and aging parents in the story of Alex and Linda.

Alex and Linda

Imagine an adult child, Alex, who is balancing a demanding job and family life while also caring for her aging parent, Linda. Linda frequently calls Alex throughout the workday with various requests and concerns, which disrupts Alex's professional responsibilities and causes significant stress.

Communicating the Boundary

Alex might approach Linda with empathy, saying, "I really want to be there for you and help you with everything you need, but I'm finding that the frequent calls during my work hours are affecting my job. To make sure I can give you the attention and support you deserve, let's set a specific time each day for us to talk and go over any concerns you have."

Maintaining the Boundary

If Linda calls during work hours, Alex could gently remind her, "I'm at work right now, so I can't take calls until our scheduled time. Please leave a message or we can discuss it during our call later today" If Linda continues to disregard Alex's stated need, Alex might take it a step further and say something like, "If you continue to call me at work, I will change my phone settings to block your calls during work hours. I prefer to stay available to you for emergencies, so my hope is that you will not create a situation where this becomes necessary. I look forward to talking with you when I can give you my full attention."

Why This Works

Alex is not telling Linda what to do. Linda continues to make her own choices. Alex allows Linda to own those choices but does not react or respond in frustration when Linda disregards Alex's clearly communicated desires. Instead, Alex lets Linda know that, should she continue to disregard these desires, Alex will take alternate steps to be sure her time and energy are respected while still setting aside time for Linda. This approach respects both Alex's professional responsibilities and Linda's needs. It sets a clear boundary with kindness and consideration. It ensures that Alex can effectively manage commitments while still providing support to Linda in a structured manner. This balance helps maintain a healthy relationship and prevent burnout from the care partner taking on too much at once.

Life without healthy boundaries can lead to a constant state of overwhelm, stress, and interpersonal conflicts. Without clear boundaries, you might find yourself overcommitting to others' needs at the expense of your own well-being. Have you ever felt this? Is this your life now? Is this exhaustion showing up when you look in the mirror?

Ineffective boundaries lead to burnout and resentment. Relationships can become strained as expectations blur and personal space erodes, causing frequent misunderstandings and emotional turmoil. The absence of boundaries can also result in you having a lack of respect for your own limits, making it difficult to prioritize self-care and maintain a balanced lifestyle. This in turn leads to feelings of being undervalued or taken for granted, as well as difficulties in achieving personal goals and maintaining a sense of identity. Can you see how being "helpful" to everyone all the time isn't really helpful at all? Without healthy boundaries, life becomes a chaotic and unmanageable series of demands and conflicts. In this state, life happens *to* you, not *for* you. If you feel like this is your life now, there's no doubt you have a heart for service. What a beautiful gift to share with others... when it is balanced. I invite you to get curious and pay attention to how quickly you say yes to people's requests and why. Are there areas where you can pull back? If so, do you feel guilt when you do? Get curious about this, too. Joy and fulfillment come from balanced and respectful interactions. You will ultimately have more to give to others when you learn the language of healthy boundaries.

FACING RESISTANCE: THE CHALLENGE OF MAINTAINING BOUNDARIES

In Chapter 2, we discussed the difference between a fixed mindset and a growth mindset. I can tell you from experience that you will wear yourself out if you expect a person with a fixed mindset to happily respect your boundaries. This does not mean you should avoid establishing boundaries with these friends and family members; just understand that the process may be more difficult. Remember—boundaries are not about changing the other person; they are about making life better for you.

We establish boundaries not to keep people out, but to create balance. If people in our lives are accustomed to our constant support, they may not easily accept it when we begin asserting our needs through establishing or reestablishing boundaries. It is especially ironic that the people with whom we most need to hold boundaries tend to be the most vocal, possibly even aggressive, about reasserting their "needs." For example, it takes courage for a woman to assert boundaries with a demanding, intimidating partner. Even with children, especially grown children, the pushback can be formidable at first.

So start small. Work on what you can, as you can. Think of it as a leveling-up game—each failure leads you closer to success. This may mean focusing on yourself for a while in order to boost your confidence a bit and rebuild enough self-esteem to make a change. Remember that change may take time. You may need to level up your communication skills to handle conversations better. Learning to say something as simple as "Let me get back to you about that" instead of immediately agreeing to requests can be a meaningful step forward. Rome wasn't built in a day, and neither are boundaries. We feel our way through this process. Some people may require several conversations to get used to the new you, and that's okay. Just start. As I've said before, small changes add up.

As you learn the skill of establishing boundaries—and it is a skill—being able to return yourself to a balanced state can be extremely helpful. The next chapter will cover this in detail.

Use the sentence stems below to define what healthy boundaries would look like in your life. Fill in each blank with the first thought that comes to mind. Give yourself grace. Establishing and maintaining healthy boundaries takes practice.

If I feel overwhelmed, I will take a break by _____

_____

_____

_____

When I notice disrespectful behavior, I will remove myself from the situation by _____

_____

_____

_____

To maintain my energy, I will limit my time spent on

_____

_____

_____

If I am not feeling heard, I will express my feelings and then _____

_____

_____

_____

In order to take care of my mental health, I will prioritize _____

_____

_____

_____

If someone tries to pressure me, I will respond by ___

_____

_____

_____

_____

When I need personal space, I will ensure I get it by _

_____

_____

_____

_____

If a conversation becomes too heated, I will _____

_____

_____

_____

_____

To stay true to my values, I will make decisions based

on _____

_____

_____

_____

If I feel my boundaries are being crossed, I will enforce

them by _____

_____

_____

_____

_____

_____

CULTIVATING SELF-CARE WITHIN CONNECTION

We all want connection. We want to love the people in our lives as best we can. But we also have a responsibility to take care of ourselves and not ask for more from each other than we can give.

There are times in life, like when we have small children, when it is necessary to set our needs aside for a while. But this is not a way to live long-term. No one benefits from us exhausting ourselves, especially in the guise of helping others. This is contrary to much of what women have been taught, either directly or indirectly, by our culture and, for some, our families. But caring for ourselves—for all of ourselves, however we need to do that—is not selfish. It is wise. It is honest. It is how we bring our best selves to our relationships so we can love fully, beautifully, as who we truly are.

Relationships can be wonderful, difficult, draining, and delightful—sometimes all at once. But we are meant to connect with others. The next chapter opens a discussion about another, perhaps even more essential, source of connection.

Chapter 7:

Honor Your Body

In the prior chapters, you learned a lot about how anti-aging does not work and how the ideas it is based on are false. You were introduced to the core principles of Thoughtful Aging. We looked at beauty in all its forms and the ways we use it, including how beauty can shape our identity and help us get attention, or help us hide behind the expectations of others.

Now I want you to be able to apply these concepts to your daily life. Up to this point, what I've given you is just information. It's knowledge. We use knowledge to make good decisions for ourselves and others. Knowledge becomes wisdom through lived experience. Put into practice, what I've shared with you will become wisdom you carry forward to enrich your life.

The promise I made to you at the beginning of this book was that, by the time you turn the last page, you would be able to see your own beauty when you look in the mirror. In this chapter, we will explore how to do that in greater depth.

I'll start by telling you how I did it.

FROM SURVIVAL MODE TO WHOLENESS

Several years ago, I was living in a state of constant discomfort. I had built a business that I was actively expanding, was parenting teenagers and young adults, and caring for grandchildren in whatever free time I could find. I was also living each day with the discomfort of low-grade headaches, nausea, back pain, shoulder pain, and bouts of numbness in my left arm, all of which I attributed to stress, not sleeping well, or the major car accident I was in when I was eight months pregnant with my first child.

I could also see the end of my marriage rapidly approaching. Years of marriage retreats, individual and couples therapy, date nights, and schedule changes could not repair the union that probably never should have been. I attacked each day with a fervent determination to succeed, fix broken relationships, and keep everyone happy along the way. I experienced intentional moments of joy, but overall, I felt alone. I began to question why I felt disconnected from everyone around me when I was so actively involved in other people's lives. I was always available for a good conversation, willing to help and show up for others when needed. I was actively seeking to live a virtuous life. Things weren't adding up.

When I finally left my marriage, my physical symptoms of discomfort went away overnight. This fascinated me. How was it even possible? Could those physical symptoms have been my body calling for my attention all those years? Were they manifested by my constant compromise of soul for the sake of harmony? Sure, I felt better, but why did I still feel disconnected? The life I had been living was not aligned with the person I knew myself to be. Did I really know myself at all? I felt lost.

Looking back, I realized that I had spent most of my life—if not all of it—in survival mode without even realizing it. My focus had always been on getting things done, accomplishing tasks, and making things work. I had this grand idea that the people in my life couldn't survive without me, that I was essential to their well-being in ways I could not afford to question.

There was a kernel of truth in that, but my ego was feeding me the lie that everybody needed me so completely that, should I take a moment for myself, their worlds might fall apart. I was so caught up in that lie that I did not once stop to consider how my giving was not helping anyone, it was harming me. I had these beautiful resources of body and soul and was ignoring both. They were doing everything they could to get my attention, but my mind was shutting them down for the sake of survival.

For example, I would get a late-night call: "Oh, you need a ride home because you can't drive? Okay. It's late, but I'll come get you." "You need a dog sitter for the weekend? I had planned on relaxing, but I can do it."

"You have concert tickets and no babysitter? I had dinner plans, but I guess I can reschedule." Don't get me wrong, I enjoy helping others. But I was not helping from a place of genuine desire. I was doing it out of a sense of obligation, always sacrificing my needs for someone else's. On the surface, this might seem virtuous. But each time I did it, the gratification I was hoping to feel through my "selfless" service was never quite enough to compensate for the sacrifices I had made.

It didn't stop there. I was hungry but wouldn't eat. I wasn't hungry and would eat. I put off bladder urges until they reached crisis mode and then rushed off to the bathroom, barely making it in time. I felt the need to exercise and promised myself I would do it later. I couldn't take a breath any deeper than my chest level. (I found out later that this is called "survival breathing.") My body was working *for* me, not *with* me, because I wouldn't allow it. My mind had been in the driver's seat for so long that my suppressed body signals were no longer recognizable as anything other than inconvenient.

This growing awareness of my disconnection was the start of my earnest search for a deeper mind-body connection. I began paying attention to the signals my body was sending and honoring them with curiosity instead of dismissal. For instance, when my back hurt, instead of heading straight for the bottle of pain reliever, I paused to reflect. What had I done that day? What could my body be trying to tell me? By creating these moments of intentional connection, I learned to welcome the messages my body wanted to share. Honoring my body through awareness was enlightening, but I still felt stuck. I was gaining knowledge, yet unsure how to apply what I was learning.

During this period of exploration, I attended a retreat where I was introduced to somatic therapy. Somatic therapy focuses on releasing stored emotions from the body by using various mind-body techniques. I had experience with conventional therapy, eye movement desensitization and reprocessing therapy (EMDR), cognitive behavioral therapy (CBT), and neurolinguistic programming (NLP), all of which had greatly contributed to my growth. I felt hopeful and eager to explore this new approach.

I engaged with a somatic therapist who helped me understand the power of breathwork and how and why the mind and body become disconnected. We don't consciously choose disconnection. It's our body's way of protecting us from the real and perceived threats we experience from childhood on. Reaction becomes a way of life. The false belief system I was holding in my nervous system was preventing me from feeling whole.

Through somatic therapy, I discovered the countless ways my body had carried the weight of my life experiences. It had supported me all along, storing emotions, trauma, and memories. For the first time, I truly felt what it meant to be connected, not just to my body, but to my emotions, my experiences, and, ultimately, to others. I realized that my internal disconnection had been the very thing blocking the deep, meaningful interpersonal connections I had always longed for. Despite my belief that I was doing everything "right"—being there for others, self-sacrificing, seeking harmony—I had been disconnected from my own inner world.

Honoring my body allowed me to reach a depth within myself where I experienced true self-compassion and grace. Any guilt or shame that I had carried about how I had parented, the state of my marriage, mistakes I thought I had made, and regrets just evaporated from my thoughts. Without the noise of codependent distraction, I was able to have conversations with my body based on gratitude and appreciation, not judgment, suppression, or frustration.

If you have ever felt complete and whole, even just for a moment, you know it's like seeing the sky on a clear day. Once you have seen it, you can't unsee it. In this case, you can't *unfeel* it. Thoughts of judgment, shame, guilt, regret, and inadequacy may still float by like clouds, but they no longer dictate your state of being. They simply come and go. That feeling of wholeness becomes your new focus.

We feel most alive in the presence of beauty, in all its forms. Beauty reconnects us to our highest selves and reminds us of the infinite potential within. Think about moments when you have felt this: being in love, holding a sleeping baby, or giving or receiving the gift of being fully present with another person. These are all experiences of beauty that bring us back to our true essence.

EXERCISE:
RECONNECT WITH YOUR BODY

I want to share some exercises with you that helped me rebuild a healthy relationship with my body. As I pursued this newfound connection with my body, I realized that I did not know how to interpret its signals. I had to create that language, and I found sentence stems to be a powerful tool. By using these prompts a few times each week, I was able to open up a deeper dialogue between my body and mind. I invite you to try that now. Fill in as many blanks as you can with whatever comes to mind first. There are no right or wrong answers, just an invitation to listen and engage.

Getting back into a relationship with my body is _____

_____

_____

_____

_____

Noticing the subtle changes in my body each day feels

_____

_____

_____

I really think I am starting to _____

_____

_____

_____

The feeling I've most noticed in my body is _____

_____

_____

_____

I'm a little cautious about exploring _____

_____

_____

_____

Honoring that awareness feels _____

_____

_____

_____

One way I could explore the edge of that is _____

_____

_____

_____

I'm afraid I might feel _____

_____

_____

_____

The last time I truly allowed myself to feel that way was

_____

_____

_____

_____

I think I could really begin to expand my capacity by

_____

_____

_____

A practice I can take up in my daily life to help with this

is _____

_____

_____

_____

_____

I give myself my word that I will _____

_____

_____

Choosing ME and trusting ME feels _____

_____

_____

_____

Acknowledging that my body holds truth and wisdom

is _____

_____

_____

When I think about growing older, I _____

_____

_____

_____

When I imagine looking at myself in the mirror in five

years, I _____

_____

_____

_____

When I imagine looking at myself in the mirror in ten years, I _____

_____

_____

_____

Me as a beautiful eighty-year-old would be _____

_____

_____

_____

I can have a wonderful, beautiful life for decades because _____

_____

_____

_____

_____

Now that you've completed this exercise, how do you feel? Unsteady? Hopeful? Inspired? No matter what feelings arise, take a moment to notice where they reside in your body. For example, do you feel a tightness in your chest or a knot in your stomach as certain thoughts come up?

When I first started these exercises, I often encountered physical discomfort in my body. At times it showed up as a knot in my stomach, a tightening in my chest, or a lump in my throat, as if I couldn't speak. Each of these sensations pointed to something deeper. Rather than avoiding the discomfort, I leaned into it, using intentional breathing to calm my nervous system. All of these feelings, which I had previously ignored, were clues to what needed attention and healing.

RESETTING WITH BOX BREATHING

Intentional breathing is key in somatic therapy, and one of the most effective techniques I have found is box breathing. It is simple and can be done anytime, whether in the morning, as you fall asleep at night, or during stressful moments throughout the day. You can do it right where you are now. Once you become familiar with the process, this technique can become one of your most valuable resources in managing anxiety and revealing your true beauty.

Getting Started with Box Breathing

Sit in a chair, stand, or lie down on your back with one hand on your chest and one hand on your stomach. If you are in a chair, be sure that your back is supported and that your feet are firmly on the floor.

Breathe as you would normally for a minute.

Observe the rise and fall of your chest and stomach.

If you notice that your chest is rising but your stomach is not, your breathing is shallow (survival breathing). If your stomach is rising, you are breathing deeply, activating full relaxation in your body.

Be aware of your breath. Ensure that you are taking deep breaths and allowing your stomach to rise.

If you are lying down or seated on a chair, you will feel your back press against the floor or the back of the chair when you take a deep breath.

If this is your first time practicing box breathing, push your stomach out while focusing on taking smooth, deep breaths.

Four Steps to Mastering Box Breathing

Step 1: Breathe in through your nose while slowly counting to four. Feel the air enter your lungs.

Step 2: Hold your breath for four seconds.

Step 3: Slowly exhale through your mouth for four seconds.

Step 4: Repeat steps 1 through 3 until your thoughts become quieter and you reach a point where you are feeling more than thinking. This returns you to a grounded, present state of beauty.

Repeat this exercise as many times as you can. Thirty seconds of deep breathing will help you feel more relaxed and in control. Even the busiest people can find thirty seconds for this exercise, and thirty seconds of box breathing is enough to decrease your stress levels and re-set. An awareness of breath and intentional breathwork will calm your nervous system enough to allow you to *feel* what is being communicated.

WHAT DO YOU BELIEVE ABOUT YOUR BEAUTY?

Once you have familiarized yourself with box breathing, you've gained a powerful tool for grounding yourself in the present moment whenever you feel disconnected or overwhelmed. Now that you are equipped with this tool, we can move forward to explore the deeper beliefs you hold about your beauty. If you feel discomfort or resis-tance as you examine these messages, remember to return to the box breathing exercises above. Give yourself grace to pause, breathe, and re-center.

You are perfect, just as you are. You may not believe this yet, but my hope is that you will by the time you reach the end of this book.

Love yourself first and foremost and stop trying to live up to what you perceive as the world's definition of beauty.

Love yourself. Try to look at signs of age as badges of honor, warrior scars earned in the battle of life.

—Survey respondent

GLAMOUR IS NOT BEAUTY

Have you considered that you may be mistaking glamour for beauty? It's easy to focus on our external appearance. It's what we see each day and how the world sees us. But the way we conduct our lives in the light of cultural expectations is what defines our beauty. Remember, though our culture is addicted to image, that does not mean we have to be, too. As I've said in previous chapters, you are your own gatekeeper. If you allow the noise of culture to continue to define your perception of your beauty, awareness of your true beauty will evade you. It will feel out of reach. But if you draw back inside yourself, you will find immense resources of thought and energy, a power each of us holds to reignite the beautiful, soulful spark that makes us who we are.

What will it take to awaken this? For many, it comes from reconnecting with things they love, like poetry, fiction, art, aesthetics, theater, dance, music, or film. What moves you? What inspires you? What stirs your soul?

Consider the conversations you have with yourself when you see your reflection in the mirror. Are they positive or critical? What do they say about the connection between your inner world and your outward appearance? Use the sentence stems below to explore your thoughts.

When I see my reflection, the first thought that comes
to mind is _____

_____

_____

_____

I feel most beautiful when _____

_____

_____

_____

The activities that make me feel alive are _____

_____

_____

_____

I would feel more connected to my beauty if I allowed
myself to_____

_____

_____

_____

If you answered these questions honestly, you may be
feeling a little lost, and that's okay. I'm asking you to be
vulnerable and explore your beauty in ways you may nev-

er have considered before. Feeling lost is a natural part of the process. When you step outside the box that has defined your life, you enter unfamiliar territory. But here's the truth I realized when I started to break away from everything I thought I knew: I was not lost, I was simply undiscovered. Without discomfort, there's little motivation to change. It is within a state of discomfort that we find new ways to grow. Embracing discomfort may feel counterintuitive, but it is a practice that can lead to transformation. What opportunity is discomfort offering you? How can it help you discover new dimensions of beauty? Use these sentence stems to explore any discomfort you may be feeling.

When I feel uncomfortable about my appearance, the deeper feeling underneath is _____

_____

_____

_____

Discomfort in my body often leads me to think about myself_____

_____

_____

_____

An opportunity discomfort might be offering me is __

_____

_____

_____

_____

The growth process I went through was extreme, and it was rapid because I was in such a state of discomfort. I'd had two "failed" marriages—failed by conventional standards, not failed if you're someone who lives to learn. Both of those marriages brought me to a new place in life. Both of them taught me many things. Who I was when I entered those relationships was not who I was when I left them. It is not who I am now. But both of those marriages and their endings made me question how I had been living.

The person you were always meant to be isn't determined by the circumstances in which you've lived. Instead, it is found in the essence of your true beauty. That's what we're working toward—reconnecting with your authentic self. But be prepared: There is a lot of external noise and internal clutter to wade through before you can get back to that core.

Before we go on, let's pause and reflect. Take a moment and write out your answers to each of these questions:

What gifts have you been given? _____

_____

_____

_____

_____

What talents do you possess? _____

_____

_____

_____

_____

What desires do you have to create good in the world
around you? _____

_____

_____

_____

_____

_____

_____

How do you express those desires?_____

_____

_____

_____

_____

As you consider your answers, are you feeling a little better about yourself? I hope so, because I think you are amazing. And I am so excited to see just how brightly your light can shine!

Doing this kind of inner work has a profound effect. As your confidence grows, you may notice yourself standing taller, your movements becoming more graceful, and your facial expressions softening, even when you're not smiling. Your eyes become clearer and brighter because you are grounded and present in beauty. You begin to see circumstances through a lens of calm confidence and feel ready for whatever comes your way. Challenges don't feel as threatening because you are pursuing your purpose, reconnecting with your true self, and becoming the person you were meant to be all along.

David Bowie said, "Aging is an extraordinary process whereby you become the person you always should have been."[30]

It absolutely can be. But it doesn't happen by accident. It takes intention, reflection, and the willingness to dig deep and return to your true beauty.

WHO ARE YOU ON VACATION?

Have you ever been on vacation, perhaps two or three days in, relaxing on a lawn chair on a beach or enjoying a meal at a restaurant, and suddenly realized that nothing else matters at that moment? All of the thoughts that had you stressed out and worried have finally gone quiet and you find yourself simply being present. With that realization, you might think, *This is nice. I should do this more often. I'm going to plan more vacations because I really love this feeling of freedom from stress or worry, the feeling of not being pulled in a hundred different directions.*

If you have had this experience, consider this: If you can feel that sense of peace while on vacation, you have the capacity to cultivate it in your everyday life as well. What is happening during those moments of relaxation is that you are not focusing on the noise around you. Instead, you are present with what is right in front of you. This is easier to achieve on vacation because the environment is different, the scenery is unfamiliar, and you have intentionally carved out time for yourself away from the chaos.

It's crucial to realize that the peace you experience on vacation isn't solely the result of your surroundings. It is not the environment that's creating that for you. It stems from your ability to step away from your routine, to give yourself permission to pause and simply be. You can be fully present while on vacation and, with some practice, you can achieve that same tranquility in your day-to-day life.

One of the quickest ways to return to the present moment is to find beauty in something around you. It could be the color of a wall, a delicate flower, a bird, or a blade of grass. We are surrounded by beauty that is just waiting to guide us back to the present moment and fill our hearts with joy. Don't believe me? Try it. Look around you. Allow yourself to get lost in the beauty of something nearby. Quiet your thoughts and immerse yourself in the present moment with whatever has your attention. Take a deep breath and truly feel it. What sensations arise? Make a mental note of these feelings and pay special attention to anything that feels familiar. This practice not only enhances your appreciation for beauty but also strengthens your connection to your true self.

Beauty is built upon the moments we create for ourselves, moments that allow us to expand in positive ways. It's our responsibility to ensure that these moments are grounded in the foundation of our character or the character we aspire to develop. The noise of daily life, the drama, and distractions, will always be there. Ultimately, it is our choice to engage with it or not. Again, we are our own gatekeepers. We don't have to accept everything that comes our way. We have the autonomy to choose what serves us best. Our beauty resides within us, waiting to be honored, but this requires conscious effort.

EXPECT PUSHBACKS–FROM YOURSELF

Embracing this journey toward self-honor and beauty can be challenging. As I mentioned earlier, change is often uncomfortable, and many people instinctively resist it. As we explore the idea of honoring our inner beauty, you may encounter what I have experienced as "pushbacks," the reasons or excuses we create to avoid discomfort. You may already have experienced some of these pushbacks while reading this book. The key question is not whether they will arise, but when they will surface. Here are the most common pushbacks you might experience, along with strategies to navigate them.

Pushback: I Don't Have Enough Time

One of the biggest difficulties of modern life is that time has become the enemy. We view time as a bully, a dictator running our lives. We are captive to it. In this sense, we become victims of it. By the end of the day, most of us have not had a moment to ourselves to just be. When we get caught up in the checklist of life—"How should I meditate?" "How should I pray?" "How should I think?" "What should I do?"—we neglect the most important question, which is, "How should I be?"

Slowing down with intentional breathing and an intentionally grounded presence helps us find our rhythm. When we come into our own rhythm, we enter a different kind of time. It pulls us out of our overstructured lives and into a space of stillness. Imagine the ocean, tumultuous on the surface but so peacefully still below. Once you slip below the surface of your life, time will no longer rule you. You will begin to see time not as the enemy, but as a resource.

Simply put: By thinking differently about time, you can begin to see it as a way to access presence. By presence, I mean the undiscovered beauty you have not yet allowed yourself to experience. The radiance that is you. Understanding this is transformative. Time goes from taking something from you to offering something to you. I'm not asking you to find more time in your day; I'm suggesting you reclaim the minutes you already have.

Pushback: My Life Is Too Stressful to Think about Change

Change can feel overwhelming, especially when life is stressful, leading many to resist the idea of transformation altogether. However, I invite you to open your mind. Your brain won't fall out, but years of conditioning will.

At our core, we all possess an incredible imagination. No matter how mature, adult, or sophisticated we may appear, at heart, we still carry within us the essence of our childhood selves, those imaginative beings who dream vividly each night. Our dreams, those complex and imaginative stories we create for ourselves, reflect our capacity to see beyond the structures we have built around our daily lives. Embracing that inner world can be a powerful source of inspiration. It is not necessary to remember our dreams to trust our capacity to change. Even if it feels diminished, your ability to dream, believe, and create is still accessible to you.

I understand that life can be complicated and stressful. The need for stress management is real. I am not suggesting that you abandon your responsibilities. I'm inviting you to consider how moments of quiet throughout your day can transform your ability to cope with stress so that it is no longer a driving force in your day-to-day decisions. Recognizing the importance of this perspective shift can have a profound effect on your spirit, well-being, and overall health. Don't wait for a crisis to occur before you get curious about this opportunity for growth. Honor your resilience as you simultaneously reawaken your capacity for change. Create space in your life for change and practice gratitude for your journey. When was the last time you felt a lightning bolt of awareness? Did it scare you or ignite your passion? There's a whole beautiful you waiting to be discovered. Chaos is constant, but peace can be, too. Choose wisely and allow yourself the grace to embrace change in the midst of stress.

Pushback: Positive Thinking Is Not Going to Change How I Look

As discussed above, it is easy to get caught up in the critical conversations we have with ourselves when we look in the mirror. How does your inner world, and the way you feel about yourself, shape the way you see your physical appearance?

Our attention naturally gravitates toward our external appearance because that is what we and the world see every day. However, true beauty is not rooted in how we look but in how we live and choose to show up despite the noise of cultural expectations. Yes, our society is obsessed with image, but that doesn't mean you need to be. If you continue to let cultural standards dictate your sense of beauty, you will always feel as though you are missing something, and beauty will remain elusive.

Are you ready to shift that inner dialogue? Start by truly accepting that beauty is not just external; it reflects how you conduct your life and embrace your unique self. I promise you: You are enough. When you see yourself from a place of inner worth, you move away from viewing your appearance through the lens of "not enough." Shift your focus to what is beautiful within you, the qualities that define you beyond your physical appearance. Reframe the narrative in your mind so that each time you look in the mirror, you challenge the negative thoughts and remind yourself that true beauty starts from within. This shift will not happen overnight, but with consistency, you will start to see—and feel—beauty as something you carry, not something you wear. As a recovering beauty-denier myself, I fully believe in your ability to see and feel your true beauty.

BEYOND THE NOISE AND DISTRACTIONS

We have the answers we need, if we can get past the noise and distractions around us. This is no small pursuit. It is an ongoing, lifelong endeavor. There are endless distractions, many of them alluring and ever-present. But until we can get quiet and reconnect with what matters, we will continue to feel disconnected from ourselves, our wisdom, and our beauty. We will chase things that don't matter and don't last. The simplest and most direct way to return to ourselves is to start listening to our bodies and finding beauty in the present moment. The next most important thing to connect with and clear is our minds.

Chapter 8:

Mindset: Quiet Your Inner Critic

Do you believe that we create our own reality? Do you think we have control over our life experiences? Can the way we perceive our experiences transform our lives? I have contemplated these questions for a long time. For me, the answer to all three questions is yes. In this chapter, I will show you exactly how I came to believe this, and how you can change your perception and your experience, too. In doing so, you will also shift who and what you see in the mirror.

The transformation I underwent did not happen by accident. It began with a powerful mindset shift. The world around me had not changed, but my perspective, the way I interpreted things around me, became entirely different. Much like a filter or smudges on the lens of a camera, when your thoughts are distorted, the picture of your life appears dull and out of focus.

As I worked to clear that lens, my attention was drawn to the constant stream of negative thoughts I had running in the background of my mind. This negative self-talk, often referred to as automatic negative thoughts (ANTs), is like a whispering shadow that follows us. ANTs don't change the reality around us, but they darken our perception of it, making things seem worse than they are. Without altering our circumstances, ANTs can profoundly affect how we interpret and respond to the world, shaping our behavior in ways that can be deeply limiting.

> **We are tremendously critical of ourselves, and society is critical of us as well. We are judged and ultimately ignored. There is a bit of a movement for women to embrace aging, although it is very challenging. We are terribly critical of and hard on ourselves.**
>
> **—Survey respondent**

Have you ever stood in front of a mirror while applying makeup or fixing your hair and smiled at your reflection while inside, a quiet voice said, *You're just trying to hide how tired and old you look?* To the outside world you might appear confident and put-together, but your inner dialogue tells a different story. Or how about when you're at a social event, laughing with friends and seemingly enjoying yourself, and yet that voice in the back of your mind is whispering, *They're only being nice because they feel sorry for you.* These thoughts, though unspoken and unproven, subtly shape your behavior. You withdraw and do not fully engage because you assume you don't fit in, even though your friends' warmth and friendliness invite you to connect. This is exactly what I struggled with before I decided to attend my friend's wedding in Italy, which I shared with you back in Chapter 2. Had I let my ANTs make decisions for me, I would not have attended that wedding. As a result, I would have missed meeting someone who later played a pivotal role in my journey and ultimately led me to find purpose through serving on the board of a nonprofit organization.

The struggle with ANTs isn't unique to me. All the women I know deal with them in some form. These little "ants" run through our minds, compelling us to see many situations through a distorted, often self-critical lens. Whether conscious or unconscious, these thoughts occur involuntarily, affecting how we interpret even the simplest events throughout the day. It is up to us to recognize their influence and actively seek to clear the lens so we can see our lives without the interference of these negative distortions. Below are some common ANTs I have heard in my conversations with women over the years:

- *I'll never be good enough.*
- *They must think I'm stupid for saying that.*
- *There's no way this can end well.*
- *I will never find a good partner.*

- *I will never overcome my depression. I just have to live with it.*

- *I can't do anything right.*

- *I'm a burden.*

- *I can't do this anymore.*

- *This is just who I am. I can't change.*

We can all fill in the blank with our own negative thoughts. When we do, we'll realize they operate from five basic categories: complaint, critique, concern, commiseration, and catastrophizing.

These distorted thoughts convince us that our flaws are more visible than our strengths and that our worth is conditional or somehow lacking. When we receive a compliment on our appearance and immediately think *They're just being polite* or *They must have noticed how much weight I've gained,* we diminish the value of the kind words and undermine our own sense of self-worth. We often do this even as we smile and quietly accept the compliment.

Once we get caught in this cycle, we create a self-fulfilling prophecy. For example, a woman who constantly tells herself *I'm not good enough* is actively yet unconsciously sabotaging her own efforts. She might hesitate to speak up in a meeting, pass on applying for a promotion, or avoid social situations where she feels she won't measure up. The circumstances themselves haven't changed—she still has the skills, the opportunities, and the invitations—but her internal dialogue convinces her that she doesn't deserve them or that she will inevitably fail.

Automatic negative thoughts do not change what's happening in our lives; they change *how we experience* our lives. It's like wearing a pair of tinted glasses that color everything we see. The world outside remains the same, but our perception of it is altered, often to our detriment.

YOUR MINDSET REALLY DOES CHANGE WHAT YOU SEE

Anyone thinking "rose-colored glasses" here? This isn't just a metaphor. A 2009 University of Toronto study provided the first direct evidence that our mood literally changes the way our visual cortex operates and how we see. Adam Anderson, a professor of psychology at the university, explains: "Specifically our study shows that when in a positive mood, our visual cortex takes in more information, while negative moods result in tunnel vision."[31]

Did you catch that? If we take in more information when we're in a positive mood, we're more likely to have a balanced view. We're more likely to see "the whole picture," both good and bad. And because we have more information, we are also more likely to see more and alternate options, interpretations, and solutions to problems.

If we're in a bad mood *and* experiencing tunnel vision, we are more likely to focus our energy on what is right in front of us and what we perceive as negative. That's exactly what I did at one point in my story: focus on my wrinkles, sagging skin, and other physical signs of aging. I did not see my true self and all the other "information" about me, only what I saw as flaws. My visual cortex shut out information and gave me tunnel vision focused on those wrinkles. I literally could not see beyond them. I could not see, or perhaps more accurately could not recognize, that my bone structure still gave my cheeks an attractive shape. My vibrant blue eyes were as alluring as ever, and my lips were still full. But I could not see any of that, much less have the perspective that my looks do not equate to my value. I certainly wasn't thinking about how I could be shifting into the best years of my life. Instead, thanks to the tunnel vision my visual cortex had created, I did not see options but remained focused on my wrinkles and other signs of aging.

So people who adopt a positive outlook—who put on those proverbial rose-colored glasses—really do experience life more positively. A positive mindset can influence not just emotional responses but even physical experiences, like how we perceive colors and visual contrasts. Essentially, how we choose to view the world can actually alter our reality, making the idea of shifting our mindset more than just a feel-good concept; it's a powerful tool for transforming our lives. It means we actually can create our own reality. We can control our experience in this life. It all comes down to our mindset.

Unconvinced? You have almost certainly heard that a positive mindset can alter your life for the better. And maybe you have tried cultivating one now and again. Maybe it is not working so well. Often when I hear talk about positive mindsets, it sounds very much like we just have to think positively and somehow, our lives will be magically reorganized. If only it were that easy!

So what does happen? When we shift into a positive mindset, we are able to see more options. We are motivated to try a little harder (yet without pushing or forcing ourselves) and we are less worn down by feelings of negativity or outright hopelessness. Simply put, having a positive mindset allows us to change our behavior. These changes in behavior are often subtle, but that is, in a way, the secret. Even subtle behavioral changes, if they are the right changes and done consistently, do change lives.

We make thousands of decisions every day. Some studies have estimated the count to be as high as 35,000 decisions a day.[32] Each one of those decisions and its tiny, almost imperceptible impact creates change. Our lives rarely change in big sweeping moments or actions. Real change typically happens in increments, often increments so small we are barely aware of them. But it happens.

Helen, the woman who made an agreement with her future self and lost a hundred pounds, did that through thousands of tiny decisions—possibly hundreds of thousands of tiny decisions. I changed my perspective on aging, revitalized my life, and was able to love who I saw in the mirror again by making a series of decisions that changed my mindset. It was a long series of decisions, but it happened. And even though ANTs are still present in my thoughts, they no longer dictate how I truly feel about my reflection.

I want to emphasize that change takes time. It takes effort. You will experience some pushback, even from yourself, as you attempt to change your thinking. This is normal and to be expected. Our job is to be ready for the pushbacks. I've included two of the most common pushbacks below. There are others—as many as there are people—but these should serve as examples to get you on your way.

I wish that I could tell you that this process is easy and that you will eventually reach the point where you no longer experience these ANTs. However, with consistency, judgment-free introspection, and an acknowledgment that these recurring thoughts exist to some degree in every woman, we can manage our ANTs better. We can reduce their frequency and learn to recognize them sooner. But first, we have to work through our human proclivity to resist change. Change, as we discussed earlier, is inherently uncomfortable. We are hardwired to gravitate toward the comfortable, even when that comfort is detrimental. ANTs will appear, and when they do, I challenge you to acknowledge them and remind yourself that you are capable, you are strong, and you are a complex, beautiful being.

PUSHBACK: IF I CHANGE MY MINDSET, WILL I BE IN DENIAL ABOUT PROBLEMS I NEED TO ADDRESS?

This is a valid concern, but shifting your mindset isn't about ignoring problems or pretending everything is perfect. Reframing your perspective allows you to see possibilities rather than limitations, strengths rather than flaws. It's about acknowledging reality but choosing to see it in a way that empowers you rather than drags you down. We do need to see the "negative" or adverse aspects of life. To ignore them in an attempt to be relentlessly positive would skew our judgment. But we can stay positive while acknowledging adversity.

Consider my story. During my worst years, I was plagued by automatic negative thoughts that influenced how I viewed myself and my life. Every time I looked in the mirror, the voice in my head would whisper thoughts like *Your neck is sagging* or *Your eyes are puffy*. These ANTs had a profound effect on my behavior. They caused me to pursue anti-aging treatments out of fear of what would happen if I didn't "fix" things rather than a desire to age well. They led me to withdraw in situations where I felt I didn't measure up.

But what if I had questioned those thoughts? Instead of accepting them as truth, what if I had asked myself, *Is this really how I want to see myself? What if there's another way to view this?* By challenging my ANTs, I could have shifted my mindset from inadequacy to self-acceptance. Rather than view my wrinkles as signs of fading beauty, I could have seen them as symbols of my life experiences, wisdom, and resilience.

Many of the women who come into my clinic are focused on superficial problems. They think that their cheeks aren't full enough or their lips are too small. Below the surface of what they perceive as deficits is a feeling of

"I'm not good enough." Even after their cheeks are fuller and their lips are larger, they still have that feeling of not being good enough. At a certain point, no matter how many products, treatments, or surgeries they get, they will have done everything they can do for their physical selves. But they may still be left feeling like they aren't good enough.

> Women have a choice. We have so much more power than we think—to be aware that each one of us has the power to live the life we want. To take time for self-care, to love ourselves always. We are in the driver's seat and [can] determine the direction we want to go and what we want to do in life.
>
> We carry radiant beauty, abundance, and wisdom inside us, all the time. Our age is just a number. We are able to do anything, even as we get much older. We can be fit, we can get our motorcycle driving license at fifty, we can take care of our body the way we see fit. That all is a choice.
>
> —Survey respondent

By shifting our mindset from "I am not good enough" to "I am capable and constantly growing," we can approach challenges with more confidence and openness, recognizing that setbacks are part of the learning process, not a reflection of our worth.

Negative self-talk is powerful, but it's not invincible. By becoming aware of it, questioning its validity, and consciously choosing to replace it with more positive, realistic thoughts, we can change not just our circumstances but how we view and respond to them. In doing so, we can transform our behavior. We can live with genuine contentment and confidence.

Pushback: What If I Can't Control My Negative Thoughts?

This fear is natural, but it's important to remember that shifting our mindset is a process, not a one-time event. It takes practice to catch and reframe negative thoughts. It's okay to stumble along the way. The goal isn't to eliminate negative thoughts entirely—that's nearly impossible—but to reduce their impact and frequency over time. Every time you choose to reframe a negative thought, you strengthen new mental pathways and make it easier to see the world through a more positive, constructive lens.

For me, this meant recognizing that my value wasn't tied to my appearance, but to the life I had lived and the wisdom I had gained. When I chose to see myself through this new lens, I found that my circumstances hadn't changed but my experience of them had. I felt more confident, at peace, and engaged with life. As a result, I took care of myself even better than I had before. I worried less and smiled more.

WHAT TYPES OF ANTS DO YOU HAVE?

Becoming aware of ANTs can be startling at first. You may feel disappointment once you realize how they have been holding you back from your true beauty. Embrace this with grace, compassion, and curiosity. It doesn't matter how they got there so much as what you will do with them now. You are the Queen of this ANT hive. First, let's explore which ANTs you have:

All-or-Nothing ANTs: Thinking that things are either all good or all bad.

Less-Than ANTs: Comparing yourself to others and seeing yourself as "less than."

Just-the-Bad ANTs: Seeing only the bad in a situation.

Guilt-Beating ANTs: Thinking in words like need, should, must, ought, or have to.

Labeling ANTs: Attaching a negative label to yourself or someone else.

Fortune-Telling ANTs: Predicting the worst possible outcome for a situation with little or no evidence for it.

Mind-Reading ANTs: Believing you know what other people are thinking.

I'll-Be-Happy-When ANTs: Arguing with the past and longing for the future.

Blaming ANTs: Blaming someone else for your problems.

REFRAMING OUR NEGATIVE THOUGHTS

Negative thoughts are automatic and habitual. According to research by Dr. Fred Luskin of Stanford University, a human being can have around 60,000 thoughts per day and fully 90% of those thoughts are repetitive.[33]

If you repeat something often enough, it creates a neural pathway in the brain. Neural pathways are like grooves in the roadmaps of our brains. The more frequently we travel a road, the stronger and more second-nature the behavior becomes. This is why negative thoughts, repeated often enough, become habitual.

Imagine what it would be like to stop criticizing yourself, to stop eroding your confidence each time you see an image of yourself or your reflection in the mirror. It would most certainly make living easier. So here is the good news: You don't have to let ANTs run your life any longer! There is a formula for getting rid of them. It takes effort and awareness, and it requires challenging and reframing the thoughts in a positive way, but it does work. Let's explore the practice of reframing using the ANTs listed above.

I'll never be good enough → *I'm constantly growing and improving. I may not be where I want to be yet, but I'm making progress each day.*

You must think I'm stupid for saying that → *Everyone has different perspectives, and I'm allowed to express mine. My thoughts and opinions are valid.*

There's no way this can end well → *This situation is challenging, but I have the strength and resilience to handle it. I can find a way to make the best of it.*

I will never find a good partner → *The right partner will come into my life when the time is right. I'm focused on becoming the best version of myself in the meantime.*

I will never overcome my depression, I just have to live with it → *Managing my depression is a journey, and I'm taking steps toward healing. I deserve support and treatment, and I believe I can find relief over time.*

I can't do anything right → *I'm human and make mistakes, but I also have strengths and successes. I'm capable of learning and improving.*

I'm a burden → *I am worthy of love and support. My needs and feelings matter, and the people who care about me want to be there for me.*

I can't do this anymore → *I'm feeling overwhelmed right now, but I've faced challenges before and made it through. I can take things one step at a time and ask for help if I need it.*

As you can see, thoughts are not facts; perception is a choice. So how do we break these habits and get rid of the ANTs? We practice. The first few times you reframe negative thoughts may feel awkward. Expect pushback thoughts like *This will never work* or *I can't get this right.* You may have to try different reframes until you hit on one that resonates with you. Keep trying. You can turn negative thinking into positive thinking. It won't be an overnight change, but rather a process that requires time, patience, and practice. After all, you have said these negative things to yourself hundreds, possibly thousands of times. You won't undo that with a quick reframing exercise. It is going to take persistence and consistency.

Write out three of your automatic negative thoughts, then reframe them.

1. _____

_____

_____

2. _____

_____

_____

3. _____

_____

_____

When I committed to reframing my thoughts, I approached it as a new habit. I adopted a simple rule: Do not say anything to yourself that you wouldn't say to a friend. I began with an awareness of my most limiting thoughts. These were the thoughts that presented themselves at the beginning of each day. I did intentional check-ins with myself throughout the day, reframing these ANTs as they appeared. This process can feel overwhelming—these are negative thoughts, after all—so I sought humor within the struggle. Most importantly, I surrounded myself with positive people. In the moments when I did not have the energy to reframe these thoughts, I turned to gratitude. Gratitude is a powerful way to temporarily quiet ANTs as you learn the art of reframing negative thoughts. I've outlined these steps for you below:

Identify Areas to Change

Pinpoint the areas of your life where negative thoughts seem to dominate. I noticed that my self-talk was particularly harsh when it came to my appearance and aging. By focusing on that one area first, I began to shift into a more positive mindset. Then I gradually expanded the practice to other aspects of my life, like my career and relationships.

Check Yourself

Throughout the day, make it a habit to pause and reflect on your thoughts. If you catch yourself spiraling into negativity, try to reframe the thought into something more positive or realistic. For instance, if you find yourself thinking *I'm not as vibrant as I used to be*, counter it with *I have a different kind of beauty now, one that reflects the life I've lived.*

Be Open to Humor

Embrace humor, even during challenging times. Give yourself permission to smile or laugh at the small absurdities of life. I found that laughter not only lightened my mood but also helped me feel less stressed and more resilient. Whether it was a funny show, a humorous conversation, or just finding the irony in a situation, I sought out moments that made me smile.

Follow a Healthy Lifestyle

Caring for your body is just as important as caring for your mind. Stay active and incorporate exercise into your daily routine, even if it is just a walk around the neighborhood. Pay attention to your diet and how it affects your moods and energy levels. Practice stress management techniques like deep breathing and meditation to maintain a balanced, positive outlook.

Surround Yourself with Positive People

Become more mindful of the company you keep. Gravitate toward people who are positive, supportive, and encouraging. Seek out friends who lift you up and remind you of your strengths. Distance yourself from those who bring negativity into your life. Surrounding yourself with positivity is crucial to maintaining your new mindset.

Through these practices, you can slowly but surely transform your thinking. I learned that while I couldn't control every aspect of my life, I could control how I responded to it. By choosing to think positively, I was able to reclaim my sense of peace, confidence, and joy.

In the end, shifting your mindset is about reclaiming your power to define your own reality. It is about choosing the lens through which you view the world. By doing that, you will transform how you feel, how you act, and, ultimately, how you live. My promise to you at the beginning of this book was that I would show you how to love who you see in the mirror, just as she is. To truly see and feel your own beauty requires letting go of automatic negative thoughts.

So, what lens will you choose today?

Chapter 9:

The True Source
of Our Beauty

Imagine a master artist whose works of art are so profound and intricate that they evoke wonder in all who behold their beauty. Each brushstroke, color, and detail is a testament to the artist's vision and skill. Now consider the world around us—the vibrant hues of a sunset; the delicate design of a flower; the vastness of the starry sky; the complexity of a human mind capable of love, creativity, and reflection.

Just as an artist's creation reveals the depth of their imagination, the beauty that surrounds us in nature is a mirror of the beauty within each of us. Whether you are someone who believes in a creator, are agnostic, or believe there is no higher power beyond us, there is no denying the splendor of our world. Imagine a butterfly landing on your hand, lying in the grass watching the trees sway in the wind, or feeling the sun's warmth as it touches your face in the morning. These moments of natural beauty gently remind us that we, too, are creations, rich with our own inner beauty and complexity that is waiting to be discovered.

Meister Eckhart, a fourteenth-century theologian and philosopher, said, "There is a place in the soul that neither time nor space nor created thing can touch."[34] No matter your biography, written across time, there is a place in you where you have never been wounded, where there is still surety, confidence, and tranquility, an inner sanctuary. Remember, we arrived here perfectly, born into an imperfect world. For those of us who have lived a life of chaos and confusion, it may be difficult to imagine that there is a quiet, still place within where peace resides and wisdom reigns. If you do not feel it now, my hope is that the words you are about to read will bring you closer to that place. I ask that you approach this chapter with an open mind and an open heart and truly reflect on what this ethereal beauty means to you.

Opening yourself to this journey requires faith, the kind of faith that trusts the energy we invest now will transform us into something greater. As with all growth, tapping into the essence of your true beauty requires both belief and practice. In time, you can become the confident woman who looks in the mirror and genuinely loves who she sees. But as you begin traveling this path, it's worth pausing to consider: What is the source of that beauty?

When I ask that question, what comes to mind for you first? Perhaps you think of God, energy, nature, faith, divinity, community, or religion and the saints therein. In the context of honoring your beauty, there is no right or wrong answer. As we move forward in this chapter together, I want us to do so in harmony. I propose that we define the source of beauty as Love. Love is the driving force behind character traits such as kindness and wisdom, acts of validation, acceptance, and self-sacrifice, and all good things.

The idea that beauty flows from Love may feel abstract, especially in a world so focused on what is visible and measurable. But perhaps by contemplating the beauty that moves us—the things that stir our souls and give our lives meaning—we can begin to see it as more than just random and part of a greater design, intentional and loving. When we see beauty this way, we realize that the gift of Love is not something we master. It is something we receive.

LOVE IS THE SOURCE OF OUR BEAUTY

Love exists in and around us. It is nurtured through spiritual development and therefore, spiritual practice can be a profound source of comfort on the path to rediscovering true beauty. Through spiritual practice, we are able to transcend external appearances and understand that real beauty is something which emanates from within. As we begin to see ourselves in a new light, we realize that the qualities that make us truly beautiful are not the ones we see in the mirror, but the ones reflected in our actions, our relationships, and our inner sense of harmony.

For those with an active spiritual life, this chapter may serve as a source of clarity and reassurance. If you have yet to explore spiritual development, my hope is you will find the following thoughts and ideas inspiring and accessible. Spiritual practices, even simple ones, strengthen our resilience. They can help us evolve and grow at any stage of life. Many people who are not necessarily religious find great comfort in their spirituality. It is both a solace and a source of inspiration. For some, spirituality is so central to their well-being that they cannot imagine life without it.

This spiritual growth doesn't just happen. While it does play a significant role in the aging process, it is a transformation we must seek to experience, much like seeing our own beauty. But before we proceed, it's important to clarify what spirituality truly means. Spirituality is not synonymous with religion. Religions are built on specific beliefs about the nature of Love, the universe, how the world began, and humanity's place within it. Religions provide a moral and ethical framework for how to live and emphasize community worship and tradition. They foster a sense of belonging and shared identity among their members.

In contrast, spirituality is based in a more individualized belief system that is open to diverse interpretations of how we experience Love. Spiritual practices focus more on meditation, prayer, journaling, seeking resources to grow through a specific challenge, or spending time in nature.

A person can be spiritual without adhering to a specific religious framework, and vice versa. Both paths can lead to profound growth, but understanding their distinctions will help guide us more clearly as we explore the connections between Love and beauty.

RELEASE OF TRAUMA

The topic of spirituality and religion may bring up memories of negative and possibly traumatic experiences for you. If so, you are not alone. Whether from a church leader, bad theology, a parent, or even a close friend, religious trauma is widespread. If this is your experience, I urge you to stop now and check in with your body. At times, memories of religious trauma have left me feeling anxious and very confused. Using the breathwork techniques discussed in Chapter 5 helped me move through these feelings. If you have experienced religious trauma, take your time with the ideas presented in this chapter. Try to stay present rather than relive the past or think about the future. There is nothing more important than this moment. Notice where you might be feeling discomfort in your body and invite Love to heal that space. Be open to whatever arises and remember to thank your body for all it does for you.

This is a gratitude prayer, or invocation, that has been helpful for me. Maybe it will resonate with you, too:

Thank you for being a home to my heart, eyes, toes, hands, and every part of me.

Thank you for the tears, smiles, and laughter that gently remind me I am human.

Thank you for the ability to love and to live.

Whatever you are feeling is completely valid. If you've experienced religious trauma, it's incredibly brave to face what you've been through, especially if it is loaded with guilt, shame, and blame that were never yours to carry.

Religious trauma leaves deep wounds, not just in how we see the world, but in how we see ourselves. Any guilt or shame you are experiencing is not a reflection of who you are. They are echoes of what others have imposed on you, systems and beliefs that were beyond your control. It's so important to recognize that while these feelings are real, they do not define you.

Healing from religious trauma is not about erasing the past, but about reclaiming your power and your right to live free of the burdens that others have placed on you. You have every right to release the guilt and shame that were unjustly given to you. They do not define you, and they do not deserve to hold you back any longer.

As you work on freeing yourself from these heavy emotions, be gentle with yourself. Healing is a journey, and it's perfectly fine to take it one step at a time. It's normal to feel angry, sad, confused, or even relieved. Each of these emotions is a stepping stone on the path to reclaiming your true self. It's okay to let go. You have the strength to release what is not yours to carry. In doing so, you open yourself up to a life where you can fully embrace who you are, without the shadows of the past.

Surround yourself with those who support your healing and understand your journey. Find spaces and people who respect your story and allow you to grow at your own pace. You are not alone, and you deserve to find freedom and joy in your life.

THE BEAUTY OF VIRTUES

Throughout this book, we have returned again and again to finding answers within ourselves rather than being distracted by the noise of the world. All the way back in Chapter 2, I shared with you how the Greek root of the word "beauty" is related to the word for "calling." I believe that a certain kind of beauty is calling to you, me, and all of us. It is calling us back to our true selves. So here we are again, turning inward, this time with an open invitation to something greater than ourselves.

Our connection to our beauty is not meant for our benefit alone. It calls us to something larger, a greater wholeness that unites us all. In its truest form, beauty is not defined by our individual thoughts, choices, or preferences. It is rooted in Love, an ever-present, unchanging force from which we are created. Even when we fail to see it, this beauty remains constant. With this understanding, let's turn our focus to defining inner virtues that allow this deeper beauty and Love to shine through.

Character

There is a structure that everyone is building, young and old alike. This structure is called character. Think of it as a house, with every single action we take adding another brick or beam. When we make choices rooted in Love, when we act with kindness, integrity, and compassion, we're not just building any old structure; we're creating something solid, something beautiful that people will recognize and admire. It's the kind of beauty that doesn't fade because it comes from within.

But just as a small crack can weaken a foundation or a single weak link can break a chain, one careless or unkind act can leave a lasting impact on who we become. That's not to say we have to be perfect, but it does mean we should be mindful of the impact of our choices. This is why every single day matters. Each time we choose Love, no matter how small that choice might seem, whether it's being patient when we're frustrated or showing kindness when it's tough, we strengthen the foundation of who we are. And as days turn into years, those small acts build up into something powerful: a life that reflects the beauty and Love we've nurtured.

Inside of each of us, there are so many forces at play: emotions, decisions, intentions—all of it. And with every act of kindness, every time we practice patience, every moment we choose Love, we contribute to the bigger picture of our lives. You may not always realize it, but with each loving action, you're shaping something that will last far beyond today.

The character we're building isn't just for the moment. It's for the future, for the legacy we'll leave behind. Think about it: Someday, when we look back on our lives, what we've built will be a true reflection of who we are. That's why the wisdom that comes from Love reminds us to be thoughtful and pay attention to who we are becoming. Because in the end, what really matters isn't the big gestures, but the little, everyday choices that shape a life of integrity and beauty.

Integrity

Integrity really is the foundation of everything that makes us truly beautiful, inside and out, because it's about being true to who we are. Sure, qualities like kindness, confidence, and grace can add to that beauty. But without integrity, those things can sometimes feel like a performance, like we're just trying to impress or gain approval. Real beauty, the kind that shines from within, has to come from a place of integrity where what we do and say lines up with our values and we live in truth every single day.

When that integrity is rooted in Love, it becomes something even more powerful. Love, in its purest form, pushes us to do what's right, even when that is hard or costs us something. It's in those moments when we make sacrifices—when we stand up for what we believe in, refuse to compromise, or tell the truth when it'd be easier to stay quiet—that our integrity really shows. That's where real beauty lies. It's not just about doing the right thing for us, but for the people around us, too.

Here's the thing: On its own, integrity can be fragile if it's not paired with wisdom. You can have the best intentions, but if you're too rigid—if you can't see the bigger picture or adapt when necessary—you can end up hurting yourself or others. Integrity shouldn't be about stubbornly sticking to rules. It's about staying true to what's right with Love and wisdom guiding you. Wisdom helps you know when to stand firm and when to be flexible, keeping you grounded in your values while still allowing you to grow.

On the flip side, wisdom without integrity is just as dangerous. You can be smart, insightful, even clever, but if you're not anchored in integrity, it's easy to manipulate or deceive others to get what you want. Sure, you might win in the short term, but without that grounding in Love and truth, what's the point? Real wisdom, when paired with integrity, is what helps us not just make the right choices, but for the right reasons, so we're always working toward something bigger than ourselves.

A woman who is known for her integrity, especially when it is grounded in Love, is someone people trust and respect. The world needs more such women: women who aren't for sale, whose hearts are anchored in truth and Love, and who will stand up against what's wrong even when it's hard and regardless of whether it's with a friend, a stranger, or even within themselves. Women with that strong inner compass can stand their ground when it feels like the world is falling apart. They can face life's challenges with grace and courage. These women are the ones whose strength comes from a Love that goes beyond just this life.

Keep in mind that integrity and honesty aren't things you gain or lose in a single moment. They're built over time, through all those small, everyday choices rooted in Love. Integrity keeps us grounded in our values, and wisdom helps us navigate life's twists and turns with understanding and care. When we have both, that's when we live lives of true, authentic beauty where Love isn't just something we feel but something we act on in every decision, no matter how big or small. And that kind of life? It doesn't just reflect our highest potential. It inspires and earns the trust of everyone around us.

Honor

Seeking true honor, the kind that reflects who we really are, is all about embracing the heart of what makes us virtuous. But let's be real: How often do we get caught up in chasing after status, titles, or just some form of public recognition? (Instagram likes, anyone?) Those things might feel good for a moment, but they're empty in the long run. True honor is about living with a real commitment to values like truth, compassion, and respect, both for ourselves and for others. Without that, we lose touch with who we truly are.

True beauty isn't just about what's on the outside. It's about finding harmony between who we are on the inside and how we show up in the world. Honor helps keep us aligned with our deepest values so that we can both give and receive Love from a place of wholeness. When

222 | THOUGHTFUL AGING

we truly honor ourselves, we set boundaries, care for our own well-being, and show ourselves some Love. And that inner respect? It shines out as true beauty, way beyond the physical stuff we usually focus on.

The ancient Romans understood this. They built temples to both virtue and honor, but the only way to enter the temple of honor was to first pass through the temple of virtue. It's such a great reminder, even today, that real honor starts with living a life of integrity. You can't just buy it or have it handed to you. It's earned, day by day, through acts of Love, kindness, and genuine goodness.

Just as beauty isn't about one feature, honor isn't about one act or trait. Being truly honorable comes from a combination of virtues, kindness, wisdom, grace, and Love. It all adds up. The Athenians understood this when they honored Aesop, a former slave, with a statue. They were showing that honor isn't about social status or how you look, it's available to anyone who lives with virtue. True honor comes from within, from living with integrity and Love.

The thing about honorable Love is that it doesn't try to manipulate or control. Instead, it invites us to be vulnerable and real. When we live honorably, we're able to Love freely and without fear of losing ourselves or compromising our values. That freedom, that ability to be vulnerable, is what lets our true beauty shine, unfiltered by what society or anyone else thinks we should be.

At the end of the day, real honor and respect aren't as hard to attain as we might think. They're earned through genuine character, not by seeking approval or relying on appearances. The most meaningful kind of honor isn't found in external rewards or recognition, but in living a life rooted in Love and virtue, knowing that true honor always comes from within.

> **We need to address our whole wellness. Not just skin, not just hair, but how we need to respect ourselves enough to take the time daily to feed our souls, our mental health, our spiritual selves.**
>
> **—Survey respondent**

PUTTING IT INTO PRACTICE: DEFINING YOUR PERSONAL VIRTUES

Character, integrity, and honor are three virtues I believe are intrinsically linked to our ability to access Love as the source of beauty. There are innumerable character traits to choose from. I encourage you to use the prompts below to determine which personal virtues matter most to you.

The virtue I value most is _____

_____

because _____

_____

_____

I believe that living with integrity means _____

_____

_____

I want to embody kindness by _____

_____

_____

I admire women who _____

_____

_____ demonstrate

_____

_____

_____ because it inspires me

to _____

_____

_____

My definition of Love includes _____

_____

_____

_____

I feel empowered when I practice _____

_____

_____

_____

The virtue of courage shows up in my life when I _____

_____

_____

To me, wisdom means _____

_____

_____ and I want to cultivate it by

_____

_____

I define true beauty as _____

_____

_____

_____

I aspire to live by the virtue of _____

_____

_____

when I _____

_____

_____

I believe that gratitude enhances my life by _____

_____

_____

_____

I want to encourage others to embrace_____

_____because

_____

_____

THE BEAUTY WITHIN

As we explore these virtues, it's essential to recognize how they lay the foundation for our spiritual awareness, revealing a world full of opportunity rather than restriction. When we embrace the belief that we can access Love, we also embrace hope. Experiencing Love brings a peace that transcends all understanding of what we know or can logically explain, allowing us to feel safe, secure, and confident in expressing our unique beauty.

Genuine beauty comes from within. This is a truth women know and embody. An AARP study of 1,992 women found that women define their beauty more in terms of who they are than how they look. They believe that attributes like kindness and their morals, character, values, and personality define their beauty more than their physical appearance.[35]

Spirituality and religion can be helpful channels to express this inner beauty, but if they do not sit well with you, let that be. Kindness alone is a wholly sufficient channel for personal growth. Find the path to your inner beauty however you can, through whatever practices work for you, at the pace that feels right to you. Be open to clues from your intuition about how to develop this beauty. It is precious, and uniquely yours. The world needs it.

Love and inner beauty are intrinsically connected to the energy source of life. Even without the context of spirituality, introspection helps us find deeper meaning. Once we begin to expand our understanding of our life's journey and the impact we have had on others, we can course-correct if we see a need for change. Or we can continue forward to create a more fulfilling and satisfying experience of aging.

SPIRITUAL GROWTH CREATES
A RIPPLE EFFECT

One person's spiritual growth can significantly benefit others in various ways. Our younger generations desperately need mentors to guide them through the changes that come with age. When we offer them guidance with our own spiritual foundation in place, we can draw on resources outside of ourselves. It's like having a whole toolbox to use when those life-changing conversations come up so we can truly support others during transitional times in their lives.

We know that leading by example is the most effective way to impact others. By seeking spiritual growth, we can facilitate healing and peace within ourselves and for others. Our personal growth, inner peace, and sense of purpose can inspire others to pursue their own spiritual journeys.

Why is this important? People who approach spiritual growth with intention usually develop greater empathy and understanding. They have a greater capacity to connect with others on a deeper level. Spiritual growth can have a ripple effect, encouraging a culture of mutual support and collective well-being. And isn't that what we are after—a collective well-being in which we uplift and inspire each other?

Moment by moment, connection by connection, our spiritual journey can have a transformational effect on society. We can nurture the Love and beauty within ourselves to strengthen our connection to the Love and beauty within others.

LOVE AND BEAUTY

Beauty is always present and available to us—the beauty of nature, the beauty of the human soul, the beauty of existence. We see it when we choose to. And when we listen, we can hear the song nature sings. The melody changes but the message remains the same: Things can always get better. Growth is inevitable. We are designed to resonate with beauty and Love. We have the free will to choose what we think, how we view our circumstances, and what we carry forward.

> We do not want merely to see beauty, though God knows even that is bounty enough. We want something else which can hardly be put into words—to be united with the beauty we see, to pass into it, to receive it unto ourselves, to bathe in it, to become part of it.
>
> —C.S. Lewis[36]

Chapter 10:

Nurturing Beauty and Well-Being Through the Decades

Many of us, especially when we're younger, fear aging. We've been conditioned to think that it means losing joy and comfort, that it's some bleak stage of life where all opportunity disappears. We dread it like we brace ourselves for winter when fall rolls around, expecting cold and gloom. But when winter actually arrives, it's not nearly as bad as we thought. It's different from the warmer seasons, yes, but it has its own kind of beauty and calm. Think of a bright winter day when the snow sparkles under the sun. The glimmers catch our attention, offering us calm and quiet moments that are every bit as wonderful as those we experience in the vibrancy of warmer seasons.

Aging is the same way. From a distance, it can feel scary, but when you get closer, you start to see the peace and even joy that comes with it. Sure, spring flowers and summer heat are gone, but there's still beauty, just a different kind. It's a beauty that's deeper, more intentional, and more thoughtful.

Our experience of aging can be like this deeper beauty, but we are more likely to appreciate it if we are intentional and thoughtful about our self-care. One of the biggest gifts we can give ourselves as we age is the commitment to keep learning, to keep growing. Educating ourselves on how to age thoughtfully, whether it's learning about health, mindfulness, or embracing new passions, lets us approach each season with purpose. In this chapter, I'll discuss the importance of skin care, aging by the decade, and the vital role hormones play in supporting healthy skin.

YOUR THOUGHTFUL AGING PLAN BY DECADE

Just as we invest in our emotional and spiritual growth, it is important to be intentional in how we care for our skin and body. If you are hoping for DIY home care suggestions, you won't find those tips here. Although I do believe natural solutions can be effective for some, I can only speak to what I know—medical-grade skin care and treatment options. I encourage you to seek out the options that are best for you. Whether you use medical-grade skin care products or at-home natural remedies, the strategy for maintaining healthy, radiant skin is to focus on prevention, protection, and correction as you age.

Prevention focuses on keeping skin healthy by incorporating products like antioxidants, retinoids, and gentle exfoliants that prevent the early signs of aging, such as fine lines and dullness.

Protection is crucial for safeguarding your skin against environmental stressors, primarily through the daily use of broad-spectrum sunscreen and vitamin C to prevent sun damage and maintain an even skin tone.

Correction involves addressing existing concerns with targeted treatments like serums that contain hyaluronic acid for hydration, peptides for firming, and ingredients like niacinamide to reduce hyperpigmentation and improve overall skin texture.

This seems like a good time to remind you that any skin changes or collagen loss you may see in your reflection are not your fault. These changes did not happen because you didn't wash your face morning and night or because you could not afford expensive skin creams. Time takes its toll on all of us. We are physical bodies bound by physical limitations. Aging happens to everyone. And that is okay. *You are perfectly beautiful, just as you are.* If there are things you would like to change about what you see in your reflection, there is no judgment. Right and wrong have no place in this conversation. Be thoughtful and intentional with how you approach aging at whatever pace works for you.

THE SKIN WE SEE–AND DON'T SEE

Each decade of aging brings specific skin changes. When I interviewed Dr. Michelle Young, a naturopath, wellness advocate, and hormone specialist, she explained it this way: "We can think of the layers of our face like we think of the structure of our bed. We have our mattress (collagen layer), we have our sheets (dermal layer), and we have our comforter (visible skin). If your mattress gets soft and saggy, you're not going to just put on a new comforter. You are going to rebuild the structure of the mattress so that the bed has more support. And maybe you have great structure and support but you have an old, flat comforter. Rebuilding the structure isn't going to help because there will still be a flat blanket on the top. When we look at ourselves in the mirror, we see a two-dimensional view. Restoring volume and supporting skin health requires a three-dimensional approach."

It is important to find an aesthetician or doctor you trust to give you a complete, thorough skin consultation. These consultations help you really understand how your skin is aging. It's a good idea to do them at least once a year, if not more often.

Etiquette tip: Many clinics offer complimentary consultations, which is great, but I recommend buying at least one product afterward. The same is true for makeup consultations at beauty stores. It's not just about supporting the business; it also shows appreciation for the time and expertise your provider has shared. And if you proceed with treatment from an aesthetician or other skin care professional, it's a nice gesture to leave a gratuity as well, if you can. It's never expected, but always appreciated and a small but meaningful way to acknowledge their professionalism.

We will dive into how to budget for treatments and procedures later on, but for now, let's take a closer look at what happens to our skin as we age, decade by decade.

> **The information below is based on my years of experience working in medical aesthetics. It should not be interpreted as medical advice but rather as a resource you can use to explore Thoughtful Aging options with your healthcare provider or skin care specialist.**

AGES TWENTY TO THIRTY

Skin

Our twenties are a decade of transition for our skin. In our early twenties, our skin is often at its healthiest and most resilient. Collagen and elastin levels are high, cell turnover is quick, and our skin retains moisture well. We may begin to notice wrinkles, but overall, our skin is typically firm, smooth, and glowing. Our skin's ability to repair itself is also at its peak. By our mid-to-late twenties, our collagen and elastin production begin to slow down, and cell turnover starts to decrease slightly. We may notice more fine lines around our eyes and a change in how quickly our skin bounces back after a late night. Cumulative sun exposure may begin to appear as sun spots, freckles, and redness in our cheeks, particularly if we do not or did not consistently use sun protection.

Our skin may start to feel drier as our body's natural production of hyaluronic acid, which helps keep skin hydrated and plump, begins to decrease. Or the opposite may happen: Hormonal fluctuations, especially those related to stress, menstrual cycles, or birth control, can increase oil production and lead to adult-onset acne or changes in skin texture.

These are the best years to incorporate medical-grade skin care into your daily routine. Good skin care is an investment. It is better to purchase one good product that works than it is to purchase three that don't work. Find an experienced aesthetician and get their recommendations. They can help you find an effective product line that works within your budget. Also recognize that your product needs may change from year to year, or season to season, as your skin begins to change.

Products to Consider

- Broad-spectrum sunscreen with both UVA and UVB blockers

- Products that contain antioxidant protection such as vitamin C

- Retinoid-based topical cream

- Weekly, at-home balancing or pore-cleansing masks

- Daily moisturizer
- Targeted lip care that contains SPF protection
- Regular exfoliation with a gentle scrub (look for a sugar-based scrub and avoid scrubs that contain plastic beads as the exfoliant, as they can damage your skin)

Treatments to Consider

- In-depth skin consultations
- Chemical peels for texture, pore size, and acne
- IPL (Intense Pulsed Light) for sun damage and age spots
- Medical-grade facials for extractions and skin balancing
- Microdermabrasion for removing dead surface skin, improving the effectiveness of medical-grade products
- Laser hair reduction
- Hormone lab draws to establish baseline levels while at their peak

Body

During this decade, our bodies undergo several changes as we move from early adulthood through the natural aging process. Bone density continues to build, reaching its peak in the late twenties. Muscle mass is also at its peak during this decade. We may notice a redistribution of body fat to different areas of the body such as our hips, thighs, or abdomen. Our sleep patterns may change due to stress, increased social activities, or starting a family. We also have a more difficult time adjusting to lack of sleep as we near the end of this decade.

Hormones

In our early twenties, our reproductive system is fully matured. Our menstrual cycles become more regular compared to our teenage years and hormonal fluctuations can influence mood, energy levels, and skin health. Contraceptives have a significant impact on the body during these years and side effects can be mistaken for "problems" that require medical treatment. I am in no way suggesting that you avoid contraceptives. That is a personal choice. I am advocating for making an informed decision. Track the physical and mental changes your body goes through and recognize that mood changes, decreased libido, acne, weight gain, headaches, nausea, cramping, unwanted facial hair growth, and more are all known side effects of oral or implanted contraceptives. Multitudes of women can attest to the fact that these side effects can have a significant impact on quality of life and mental health. They also often fly under the radar. We are so wired to internalize our discomfort that we often don't correlate what we're feeling internally with an external source. I tried birth control pills in my twenties and quickly found myself questioning my own sanity. I felt so out of touch with who I knew myself to be and couldn't make sense of the sudden change. Eventually, I recognized the correlation between my mood changes and birth control and determined that the price of my sanity was not worth the benefit of birth control.

Weight

As we progress through our twenties, our metabolism gradually begins to slow down. This results in a decrease in our basal metabolic rate (the amount of energy expended during periods of inactivity), which means that our bodies burn fewer calories while at rest. For some women, it becomes easier to gain weight compared to their teenage years; for others, it becomes more difficult to lose weight. This is when many of us form an unhealthy relationship with food and diet culture. This is also the decade in which we begin to suppress our body's signals, becoming detached from the signals we receive rather than integrating them as messages to support a healthy mind-body connection.

Nutrition

The importance of nutrition in this decade of life cannot be understated. It lays the groundwork for long-term well-being. We all know about a balanced diet of fruits, vegetables, whole grains, lean proteins, and healthy fats, and we all have felt the constraints of time and money in choosing whole foods to prepare at home. Any effort to eat well is better than no effort. Mindful eating is key, and staying hydrated is essential for navigating the physical and emotional changes that occur during these years. A good multivitamin will go a long way toward supporting any nutritional gaps. Request lab work from your doctor to determine if you need any additional supplements. Before starting any new supplement regimen, it's important to consult with your healthcare provider to assess your individual needs and avoid potential interactions with other medications or supplements you may be taking.

AGES THIRTY TO FORTY

Skin

According to UCLA Health, the body's collagen production decreases by 1% per year beginning in early adulthood.[37] With collagen playing a major role in our skin's structural integrity, it's more important than ever to be aware of how we are aging. You could be entering this decade with as much as 5–10% collagen loss. During these years, most women begin to notice more prominent wrinkles, skin laxity, and volume loss in lips, cheeks, and especially around the eyes. Skin may become rougher and less elastic, with slight sagging around the neck. While collagen loss and environmental stressors do play a role in skin changes, hormonal fluctuations are also a contributing factor. Combining a topical Poly-L-lactic acid (PLLA) bio-stimulator to a microneedling procedure will support your body's own collagen production.

Schedule an in-depth skin care consultation with your aesthetician to track any changes and consider options for maintaining or improving your skin's health and appearance.

Products to Consider

- Broad-spectrum sunscreen with both UVA and UVA blockers

- Serums targeting specific issues such as hyperpigmentation, cell turnover, and hydration

- Products that contain antioxidant protection, alpha hydroxy acids (AHAs), vitamin C, elastin, peptides, and niacinamide

- Products with retinoids (which stimulate collagen production)

- Weekly, at-home hydration or balancing masks

- Daily moisturizer that contains peptides and antioxidants

- Targeted lip care that contains SPF protection

- Regular exfoliation with a gentle scrub (look for a sugar-based scrub and avoid scrubs that contain plastic beads as the exfoliant)

Treatment Recommendations

- Radio frequency microneedling for tone, texture, and tightening
- Poly-L-lactic acid for collagen support and overall glow
- IPL (intense pulsed light) therapy for sun damage and age spots
- Neurotoxins like Botox or Dysport for wrinkle reduction and prevention
- Dermal fillers to restore facial volume

Body

Between the ages of thirty and forty, our bodies undergo even more change. If we haven't been tracking our natural aging processes, hormonal fluctuations and changes in body composition may come as a surprise. In this decade, it is more important than ever to focus on strength training for muscle mass development. Hydration remains critical for controlling weight and body function, getting good sleep, and maintaining energy levels. A good way to stay hydrated is by drinking a minimum of half your body weight in ounces of water each day.

Hormones

I cannot stress how important it is to get a hormone lab panel done during this decade of change. Again, we are establishing a baseline for what changes are to come. We are now a decade away from the peak hormone state we experienced in our twenties. We likely notice a decrease in energy, loss of focus, more prominent mood swings, and changes in our menstrual cycles. It's a good time to integrate stress-reducing activities into our daily routines. Life feels stressful when we step outside the present moment and lose sight of the beauty in ourselves and the world around us. Creating moments of stillness within through activities such as yoga, meditation, running, gardening, baking, singing, and playing music becomes vital to our ability to age well.

Weight

During this decade, our metabolic rate continues to decline, making it easier to gain weight and harder to lose it. The dreaded "diet and exercise" conversation becomes very real. What we put in our bodies has exponentially greater consequences. Portion size matters, and we may find ourselves eating when we are not hungry. Weight tends to accumulate around our midsections as we approach our forties, due in part to declining hormones.

Nutrition

Nutrition continues to play a crucial role in managing the aging process and preparing our bodies for the changes that occur during this decade. As muscle mass naturally begins to decline, protein becomes essential for preserving lean muscle mass, supporting tissue repair, and helping us feel fuller longer, which can aid in weight management. Bone density begins to decrease more rapidly, increasing the risk for osteoporosis later in life.

Eating calcium-rich foods is the best way to increase calcium; however, a good multivitamin formulated for your age group will help fill in nutrition gaps. Check with your medical provider on whether you need additional supplements such as vitamin D, B vitamins, omega-3s for supporting brain function and fluctuating hormones, and fiber, among other things.

Some of the best supplements you can take for overall skin and body health are antioxidants. Antioxidants help combat oxidative stress, which accelerates aging and increases the risk of chronic diseases. They support skin health, reduce inflammation, and protect cells against environmental damage. Outside of supplements, antioxidants are found in foods such as berries, citrus fruits, leafy greens, carrots, nuts, seeds, green tea, and dark chocolate. Before starting any new supplement regimen, it's important to consult with your healthcare provider to assess your individual needs and avoid potential interactions with other medications or supplements you may be taking.

AGES FORTY TO FIFTY

Skin

We experience significant changes in our skin in our forties, often because of the onset of perimenopause and, for some, the transition into menopause. We'll discuss these in more detail below. As estrogen levels decline, collagen and elastin production decrease significantly. Dr. Michelle Young likens the effects of this decline to baking a cake: "You can have all the ingredients—collagen, all the amino acids, all the vitamin C, the building blocks—but if you don't have an oven, you're not going to have a cake, you will just have batter. Estrogen is the oven. Taking all the supplements is not going to hurt, but all you will have is batter, not cake. When we lose collagen, we lose the ability to retain moisture. And what do women experience most in menopause? Vaginal dryness."

The loss of moisture in the skin also contributes to the appearance of wrinkles and fine lines, particularly around the eyes, mouth, and forehead. This dry skin becomes thin and prone to irritation and sensitivity. You may also notice age spots and hyperpigmentation, especially on the face, hands, and décolletage, because of sun exposure and hormone changes. Remember the bed metaphor above? This is when you begin to think you may want a new comforter.

While there is nothing wrong with this natural progression of aging, this is the decade when women really notice changes in their appearance. They no longer look as young as they feel. If you are considering preventative treatments, either through cosmetic procedures or at-home care, you don't want to wait much longer. Quite simply, you will gain and be able to maintain the most correction for the least amount of money during this decade. Think of what happens to a raisin when you soak it in water. It goes from hard and wrinkled to soft and plump. Your skin is much the same. It is essential to incorporate medical-grade skin care into your daily routine at this stage. And, of course, schedule another in-depth skin care consultation with your trusted doctor or aesthetician.

Products to Consider

- Broad-spectrum sunscreen with both UVA and UVA blockers

- Serums targeting specific issues such as hyperpigmentation, cell turnover, and hydration

- Products that contain antioxidant protection, alpha hydroxy acids (AHAs), vitamin C, elastin, peptides, and niacinamide

- Products with retinoids (which stimulate collagen production), weekly, at-home hydration or balancing masks, and hydrating moisturizers that contain ceramides, glycerin, peptides and antioxidants

- A facial oil to replenish moisture at night

- Targeted lip care that contains SPF protection

- Regular exfoliation with a mild AHA scrub that can improve radiance and skin turnover (look for a sugar-based scrub and avoid scrubs that contain plastic beads as the exfoliant)

Treatment Recommendations

- Radio frequency microneedling for tone, texture, and tightening
- Poly-L-lactic acid for collagen support and overall glow
- IPL (intense pulsed light) therapy for sun damage and age spots
- Neurotoxins for wrinkle reduction and prevention
- Dermal fillers to restore facial volume
- Ultrasound therapy for lifting
- Radio frequency thermal treatments for tightening
- Thread lifts
- Laser skin resurfacing
- Platelet-rich plasma
- Growth factors
- Radio frequency vaginal tightening

Body

Our decline in estrogen levels accelerates bone density loss, increasing the risk of osteoporosis. Hormonal changes can cause changes in breast size, shape, and firmness. Regular mammograms are essential for early detection of any abnormalities. As noted above, many women experience vaginal dryness and a decrease in libido. Sleep patterns are disrupted, and a consistent sleep schedule becomes important in establishing a healthy aging pattern. This is the decade to also begin monitoring bone density, blood pressure, thyroid, estrogen, and testosterone, and scheduling regular health screenings. And, of course, get a full lab panel as a baseline for this period of aging.

This is also the decade when most women begin to notice the appearance of gray or white hair. There's a conversation to be had about this for sure. When I see a woman embracing her natural hair color changes, I see beauty and confidence. I firmly believe that we will all have our moment when we see our gray or white hair as enhancing our appearance, not detracting from it. As with cosmetic treatments, this is a personal decision. If we are truly going to step away from beauty-based judgments, we can begin by examining why we cover our gray. Is it from a place of *want* or a place of *need?* Is it to fit in and belong or because it truly does represent a personal choice? Gray hair is not ugly, it just is. And the closer we come to seeing our true beauty, the closer we will be to embracing all the gifts aging has to offer us, whether we choose to color our hair or not. If you're considering going full gray, ask your hairdresser about how to best manage the transition. If you are unsure, an online search of Silver Sisters will reassure you that there are thousands of women all over the world who are going gray, white, or silver without shame.

Hormones

If you've not yet experienced a night sweat or hot flash, get ready... they're coming. Perimenopause, the transitional period before menopause, brings significant hormonal fluctuations, including a noticeable decline in estrogen and progesterone. This presents as irregular menstrual cycles, hot flashes, night sweats, mood swings, and sleep disturbances. Perimenopause can last for years. Menopause, on the other hand, is the time that marks the end of your menstrual cycle. Essentially, you are officially in menopause once you've gone twelve months without a period.

According to an article published by Johns Hopkins University, although the average age of menopause is fifty-one, menopause can actually happen any time from the thirties to the mid-fifties or later. It is natural and normal and nothing to be afraid of (although the symptom list below sounds terrifying). It is caused by a natural decrease in hormone levels. Women who smoke and are underweight tend to have an earlier menopause. Women who are overweight often have a later menopause.[38]

If you don't like the idea of enduring hot flashes, night sweats, vaginal atrophy, painful sex, urinary incontinence, vaginal prolapse, intermittent dizziness, cardiac palpitations, thinning hair, mood swings, depression, irritability, brain fog, or any other symptoms of perimenopause and menopause, consider talking to your medical provider about bioidentical hormone replacement, including testosterone.

While this may seem controversial, significant research has been done to debunk the myth that hormone replacement is dangerous. I urge you to do your own research and decide if flowing through menopause symptoms with the support of hormone replacement is right for you. Many women have already decided that they will never take hormones. My mother and sisters fall into this category. There is no right or wrong way to do this. It is a personal decision that women make for reasons all their own. My only request is that we, as women, make informed decisions based on science, not a medical provider's lack of knowledge or our fear of the unknown. Women who are perimenopausal, within ten years of their last period, or under sixty are usually the best candidates for hormone therapy.

Weight

The menopausal transition period in women is strongly associated with weight gain, especially in the abdominal region. Menopause specialist Jean Marino, CNP, explains it this way. "Research tells us that the number one reason for increased belly fat is a decrease in physical activity, but for women in the menopause transition, there are almost always other factors at play, including hormonal changes, stress levels, dysfunctional sleep patterns, and some medications."

She goes on to explain that testosterone is produced by the ovaries and adrenal glands in small amounts throughout a woman's life. When estrogen levels drop in menopause, the amount of available testosterone increases, which can trigger a redistribution of body fat, often causing accumulation in the abdominal region. In addition, less estrogen causes a decrease in leptin (a natural appetite suppressant) and, when sleep patterns are disrupted, an increase in ghrelin, a hormone that signals hunger and prompts the body to hold onto excess weight.[39]

What are our options? The same as they have always been... diet and exercise. When the metabolism slows during menopause, it's a good time to cut back on calories to avoid weight gain. A largely plant-based, low-fat diet with minimal processed foods is advised.

Increasing physical activity through strength training will help build lean muscle mass and protect bones. If your schedule doesn't allow for time at the gym, using ankle weights and hand weights at home can help prepare you for the next decade of life.

Nutrition

For women between the ages of forty and fifty, nutrition becomes increasingly important as the body prepares for the changes to come. Focus on a balanced diet rich in whole foods, with an emphasis on lean proteins, healthy fats, and plenty of fruits and vegetables, much as in the previous decade. Consider incorporating more plant-based meals, which can help reduce inflammation and support heart health. If you are not taking a good multivitamin, now is the time to start.

Calcium and vitamin D are essential for maintaining bone density, so ensure that you're getting enough of them through diet or supplements. Omega-3 fatty acids, found in fish, flaxseeds, and walnuts, are beneficial for brain health and reducing menopausal symptoms. Additionally, staying hydrated and managing portion sizes can help maintain a healthy weight as metabolism slows. Before starting any new diet or supplement regimen, it's important to consult with your healthcare provider to assess your individual needs and avoid potential interactions with other medications or supplements you may be taking.

Preparing for the next decade also means being mindful of stress and its impact on eating habits. Strive to practice mindful eating and consider integrating stress-reducing activities like yoga or meditation into your routine.

AGES FIFTY TO SIXTY

Skin

The goal with skin care during this decade is correction and prevention. By correction, I mean really noticing what your skin needs to remain strong and healthy. Is it dehydrated, dry, sensitive, damaged by the elements, or losing firmness? Do you have broken capillaries (red veins) around your nose or cheeks? Have you noticed a new mole or age spot that looks suspicious? Because the loss of estrogen after menopause wreaks havoc on our collagen and elastin production, your skin may appear thinner and more fragile, particularly around the eyes, mouth, and neck. Love them or hate them, you will definitely notice more wrinkles. The fat pads beneath the skin, particularly in the cheeks and under the eyes, will lose their volume as they diminish with age. Sun damage becomes more evident, especially on the face, hands, and décolleté, and the skin takes on a crepey texture. Sunscreen is now nonnegotiable and should be part of your daily routine. Protecting your skin from UV damage is crucial at any age, but it becomes even more important as the skin becomes more vulnerable. Use a sunscreen with SPF 50 or higher that blocks both UVA (aging rays) and UVB (burning rays). Consider having mole mapping done with a dermatologist so that suspicious moles and age spots do not get missed.

Products to Consider

- Broad-spectrum sunscreen with both UVA and UVA blockers

- Serums targeting specific issues such as hyperpigmentation, cell turnover, and hydration; alpha hydroxy acids (AHAs), elastin, and niacinamide

- Firming creams that contain retinoids (which stimulate collagen production)

- Growth factors to help rebuild skin thickness and elasticity

- Weekly, at-home hydration or balancing masks
- Hydrating moisturizers that contain ceramides, glycerin, peptides and antioxidants
- A facial oil or night cream to lock in moisture at night
- Targeted lip care that contains SPF protection
- Avoid harsh cleansers and exfoliants and opt for gentle, nourishing products

Treatment Recommendations

- Radio frequency microneedling for tone, texture, and tightening
- Poly-L-lactic acid for collagen support and overall glow
- IPL (intense pulsed light) therapy for sun damage and age spots
- Neurotoxins for wrinkle reduction and prevention
- Dermal fillers to restore facial volume
- Ultrasound therapy for lifting
- Radio frequency thermal treatments for tightening
- Thread lifts

- Laser skin resurfacing
- Platelet-rich plasma
- Growth factors
- Skin resurfacing
- Radio frequency vaginal tightening
- Hair growth supplements
- Supplements to support brain health

Body

By this stage of life, our bodies have undergone significant changes, both positive and negative. We've made it through, or nearly through, menopause, which can feel like a relief. No more period means freedom! Freedom from cramps, bloating, mood swings, and the plain and simple inconvenience of it all. With that out of the way, we can focus on prioritizing bone health, resistance training for healthy muscle mass, staying physically active, and monitoring body composition. Incorporating more stress-relief practices to support our mental and emotional well-being will prepare us for any health challenges we may face in the future.

Hormones

Our hormonal landscape has drastically changed by this stage. Estrogen levels drop significantly after menopause as the ovaries no longer produce this hormone in the same quantities. This decrease affects many areas and may put us at risk for certain health conditions, including those related to bone density, heart health, and definitely skin elasticity. This drop in estrogen may also cause hair to thin or become brittle. Women in general may experience an increased risk of osteoporosis, cardiovascular disease, and noticeable changes in skin texture and appearance. Progesterone, which helps regulate the menstrual cycle, also drops to low levels post-menopause. Meanwhile, declining testosterone levels affect energy levels, libido, and muscle mass. You may also have a higher risk of urinary tract infections due to vaginal dryness and discomfort during sex, not to mention bladder leaks. These symptoms do not have to become a way of life. You have options such as nonsurgical vaginal rejuvenation, vaginal estrogen therapy, and over-the-counter lubricants and moisturizers, among other things. All of these changes can be managed with a proactive approach to aging.

Weight

By the time you reach your fifties, your slower metabolism—combined with hormonal shifts—will most likely lead to weight gain, particularly around the abdomen, even if your eating habits remain the same. Continue to focus on strength training, yoga, meditative practices, and other activities that keep you moving and stretching. Keep in mind that muscle burns more calories than fat, so losing muscle can further slow metabolism and contribute to weight gain. Weight loss efforts can sometimes result in losing almost as much muscle as fat. Reduced muscle mass not only makes weight management more challenging but also affects strength, mobility, and overall physical function. The added stress of possibly caring for aging parents or dealing with work-related demands can lead to stress eating or irregular eating habits, further contributing to weight gain. Stress, especially, can increase levels of cortisol, a hormone that promotes fat storage.

Nutrition

Focus on a nutrient-dense diet, pay attention to portion sizes, and limit processed foods, sugars, and refined carbohydrates. Your diet should have enough protein to support muscle maintenance and repair and incorporate healthy fats to help manage hormone levels. Poor sleep can disrupt hormones that regulate hunger and appetite. Make every effort to get at least seven to eight hours of quality sleep each night. Adjust your caloric intake to match your body's needs.

Addressing any challenges with targeted lifestyle changes will help you feel more confident as you navigate this stage of life.

AGE SIXTY AND BEYOND

Skin

In the early sixties, your skin may become thinner, drier, and more prone to bruising due to reduced collagen production and decreased oil gland activity. Age spots, wrinkles, and sagging are likely more noticeable. Hair may continue to thin and lose pigment, becoming a beautiful gray, silver, or white. These changes will intensify as you progress through your sixties and beyond. Gentle skin care routines focusing on moisture and skin barrier protection can help manage these changes. Vision changes may make it more challenging to notice skin changes, so be sure to schedule regular visits to assess skin health.

Products to consider

- Broad-spectrum sunscreen with both UVA and UVA blockers

- Serums targeting specific issues such as hyperpigmentation, cell turnover, and hydration

- Alpha hydroxy acids (AHAs), elastin, and niacinamide

- Firming creams that contain retinoids (which stimulate collagen production)

- Growth factors to help rebuild skin thickness and elasticity

- Weekly, at-home hydration or balancing masks

- Hydrating moisturizers that contain ceramides, glycerin, peptides, and antioxidants

- A facial oil or night cream to lock in moisture at night

- Targeted lip care that contains SPF protection
- Avoid harsh cleansers and exfoliants and opt for gentle, nourishing products

Treatment Recommendations

- Radio frequency microneedling for tone, texture, and tightening
- Poly-L-lactic acid for collagen support and overall glow
- IPL (intense pulsed light) therapy for sun damage and age spots
- Neurotoxins for wrinkle reduction and prevention
- Dermal fillers to maintain facial volume
- Ultrasound therapy for lifting
- Radio frequency thermal treatments for tightening
- Laser skin resurfacing
- Platelet-rich plasma
- Growth factors
- Radio frequency vaginal tightening
- Hair growth supplements

- Supplements to support brain health

Body

Some women may start to notice minor changes in memory and cognitive function, such as difficulty recalling names or multitasking. While mild cognitive changes can be part of normal aging, it's important to monitor these changes. Engaging in mentally stimulating activities, socializing, and maintaining a healthy lifestyle can help preserve cognitive function. If significant memory loss or confusion occurs, don't be afraid to seek medical help. Listen to the friends and family around you who are aging with you. They may notice changes which do not seem apparent to you. Above all, flow with the changes that aging brings. The transition from working to retiring, changes in your daily routine, and finding a new role or purpose can bring a sense of freedom if you stay present and curious during these changes. Loneliness can be a concern, so staying connected is key.

Regular health screenings, including mammograms, bone density tests, cholesterol checks, and colonoscopies are essential to catch potential issues early. Staying on top of vaccinations, such as the flu shot and shingles vaccine, is also important. Remember, you know your body best. Stay vigilant with preventive healthcare. Manage any chronic conditions and stay informed about new health risks through conversations with your healthcare provider and self-education.

Hormones

Bioidentical hormone therapy for women over 60, particularly those who started hormone therapy during perimenopause or menopause, has shown benefits in addressing symptoms of hormone decline and protecting long-term health. It is generally not advised to start hormone therapy after menopause or after age 60. If you are on hormone replacement therapy during perimenopause or menopause, some medical providers will tell you that you must stop hormone therapy after menopause. This may not be true for you. Studies indicate that hormone therapy, including bioidentical estrogen, helps prevent osteoporosis by slowing bone density loss and reducing the risk of fractures. This is particularly important for postmenopausal women, as estrogen depletion accelerates bone thinning. Additionally, hormone therapy may help protect cardiovascular health, another key concern in postmenopausal women, when started early in the menopausal transition.

The risks and benefits of continued hormone therapy should be personalized, based on individual health history and in consultation with your medical provider.

Weight

You may find yourself becoming less active due to retirement, lifestyle changes, physical limitations, or health issues. Emotional eating can also become more pronounced in the sixties as you navigate life changes. Engage in regular strength-training exercises to build and maintain muscle mass. This helps boost metabolism and counteract muscle loss. Aim for at least two to three sessions per week and focus on major muscle groups. Resistance bands, light weights, or body-weight exercises are effective options. Eating smaller, more frequent meals can help manage hunger and stabilize blood sugar levels.

Nutrition

Again, maintaining a balanced diet that is rich in nutrients such as calcium, vitamin D, and omega-3 fatty acids supports bone and heart health and overall well-being. Regular physical activity, including both aerobic exercises and strength training, helps maintain muscle mass, mobility, and cardiovascular health. As your body continues to age, it's important to adapt exercise routines to any physical limitations while staying active. A focus on balance and flexibility exercises can help prevent falls. Nutrition should continue to prioritize bone health, weight management, and the prevention of chronic diseases.

Try new hobbies and activities that you may have been putting off, like dancing or painting. Join a social club and stay active within your community. Emotional resilience can grow with experience as you adapt to changes and develop new coping strategies. It's likely that you will experience a greater sense of peace by focusing more on what truly matters to you.

BUDGETING AND ADDRESSING TREATMENT COSTS

Investing in quality skin care and cosmetic treatments is more than just a luxury—it is a proactive approach to maintaining your skin's health and supporting your confidence in your appearance over time. While the upfront costs of medical-grade skin care products and treatments may seem steep, they offer long-term benefits that far outweigh the expense of neglect.

Without proper care, skin issues like premature aging, sun damage, and loss of elasticity become expensive to correct later on. Effective products help you preserve your natural beauty in a more gradual and gentle way. If your goal is to feel your best at any age and to age on your terms, don't be afraid to seek advice from a professional. You don't have to buy everything they suggest—but do make sure you make informed decisions about your skin. Also, look into some of the financial strategies available to help make these investments more affordable. Pretax health accounts, payment plans, or package deals are several ways to minimize financial strain. Let's explore some of these options.

HSA/FSA: Do you have a pretax health savings or flexible spending account? Many dermatologic and medical aesthetic procedures and products can be covered by these pretax dollars. If your employer offers a matching program, this is a great way to budget for preventive care. Most plans renew in November for the following year. I always suggest scheduling a consultation prior to November 30 so that you can create a Thoughtful Aging plan for the following year and explore what treatments may qualify for payment or reimbursement through your HSA or FSA. This is a great way to cover the costs of teen acne treatments.

Payment Plans: Most clinics will offer a payment plan through a third-party financing company. These are often interest-free and extend payments out for three months to as long as twenty-four months, in some cases. Most are not solely based on credit, and many will not affect your credit with a "hard" credit pull. You may apply online or in-office and increase financed amounts as needed.

Package Discounts: Always ask about package discounts or cash-pay discounts. Because aesthetic services are best done in packages of three or more, clinics are willing to discount a multiple-treatment package. They may also be willing to offer a small discount for cash payments, which would otherwise go toward credit card processing fees.

Membership Programs: Membership programs may offer significant discounts, but not all clinics offer them. Membership benefits typically include discounts on all services and packages with no need to wait for a monthly special or holiday sale.

OUR BEAUTY BENEFITS FROM PLANNING AND INFORMED DECISION-MAKING

Aging with grace and confidence requires not only thoughtful care, but also strategic planning. Here is a summary of what you need to know: In your twenties, focus on sun protection and establishing a consistent skin care routine. In your thirties, incorporate treatments that boost collagen and target early signs of surface damage. By your forties, prioritize hydration and consider noninvasive procedures for maintaining elasticity. Your fifties, sixties, and beyond are about deep nourishment, choosing treatments that restore volume (if desired), and embracing your evolving beauty. Across every decade, making informed decisions helps you age on your terms. A key aspect of making informed decisions is knowing who to talk to and what questions to ask.

In the next chapter, we will discuss how to create a Thoughtful Aging plan and the benefits of creating a team of longevity providers to support you.

Chapter 11:

Create Your Thoughtful Aging Plan

This chapter covers the last step toward taking the knowledge you've gained by reading this book and turning it into experience and wisdom. Hopefully, by now, you are confident that:

- Our later years have the potential to be the best years of our lives.

- Our value and worth are not tied to our looks.

- Beauty and aging are wholly compatible.

- True beauty comes from our connection to our authentic selves.

- We can choose how we approach aging without judgment of self or others.

You have seen enough to know that aging can be a positive experience. But that does not necessarily happen on its own. Just as we have to be intentional about our emotional, personal, and spiritual growth, we have to be intentional about how we care for our physical bodies as we age. And so, we inform ourselves. We seek out specialists. We plan a program of action and stick to it *as best we can.*

Women between the ages of forty and seventy can benefit especially from an intentional plan for self-care because there are so many changes happening in our lives. Change can be challenging, yes. But it is always an opportunity. It shakes us loose from our old patterns and invites us to become more adaptable. Challenges, well met, can be huge confidence builders. We can meet these challenges with grace, panache, and success—especially if we embrace our old friend curiosity.

We are in a phase of redefining ourselves in these middle and later years. We don't care about the same things we obsessed over in our twenties or thirties. Not caring so much about those things brings us a sense of freedom. It lets us redirect our energies, skills, and wisdom toward different goals. We are also reevaluating relationships during this time. We see life differently and we see ourselves differently, too.

So let's circle back to two other key ideas we touched on earlier: First, that aging does not have to be a period of decline, and second, its sister idea, that we do not have to be helpless in the face of the physical downsides of aging. Whether these physical changes are wrinkles or weight gain, high blood pressure or hormone imbalances, we have choices about how to handle them. We do not have to simply sigh and say, "Well, that's just aging. It's inevitable." Certainly, aging is inevitable. Aging poorly is not. We are responsible for our care. This final chapter is all about how to be proactive in your care so you can make the most of your later years.

This is not a one-size-fits-all approach. When it comes to medical care, especially, what works for one woman may not work for another. It takes time and attention to assess what's best for us. That is something the conventional medical system just does not have the capacity to do in a fifteen-minute appointment. Let's set aside our opinions of the healthcare system and focus on what we *can* do rather than what we can't.

For starters, maybe it's time we lowered our expectations of what the traditional medical model can offer us. Instead of trying to fit ourselves into their system, let's figure out how to make their system fit into our aging process and way of life. When we reframe it like that, we become our own advocates. We are no longer dependent on a medical model that does not work for us.

I'm not a fan of the word "empowered," but I'll say it: You're more empowered when you see the conventional healthcare model as just one tool in a larger toolbox. Thoughtful Aging is about using everything available to you to feel good, be healthy, look great, and stay relevant.

This approach also asks us to adjust our expectations of our providers. If your doctor is a psychologist, you're not going to them with your concerns about blood pressure, right? We understand that specialists have their roles, but some of us have been trained to expect our primary care doctors to talk to us about all things female. More often than not, this isn't their area of expertise. And that's okay. We have other practitioners we can go to, like maybe a naturopath, gynecologist, or functional medicine doctor trained in finding the root cause of illness rather than just treating symptoms. Being proactive about your healthcare is about building a team of providers who work well together and understand that *healthcare is a service industry.* Healthcare providers are here to serve us and work *with* us.

For decades, doctors have been seen as the authority, and we, the patients, have just received their wisdom. That's not how it should be. For the majority of doctors, it is easier to tell patients what to do and have them follow orders without question. But that doesn't work. If it did, every patient would heal perfectly just by following orders, with no complications or setbacks. Medicine, like the human body, is complex and dynamic. Navigating the challenges presented with age requires collaboration between patient and provider.

In life, we build teams around us all the time. As parents, we have teachers, coaches, tutors, even grandparents helping us raise our kids. We can approach the medical system the same way. We don't have to go through life, or healthcare, alone. But to build a team, we must define what we want our optimal aging experience to be so we can gather our players. Once we have defined our optimal aging experience, we can establish relationships with longevity providers who will support our Thoughtful Aging plans.

WHAT WOULD OPTIMAL AGING LOOK LIKE FOR YOU?

I wanted to know how women define "optimal aging," so I asked them in my research for this book.

The answers I received were varied. Quite varied. And that proved one of the points we've covered several times: There is no singular optimal aging experience. That said, I did see trends in the responses I received about what "optimal aging" means. These were the common themes:

Skin Improvements

This book is focused on the topic of appearance and aging, but even without prompting women about their appearance with this question, they mentioned taking care of their skin more than anything else. Some women talked about getting cosmetic procedures. Some talked about cosmetic surgery. But most talked more generally about taking care of their skin, whether that was with sunscreen or a good overall skin care routine.

Aging Gracefully

This was the second most frequently mentioned goal. Most women did not go into detail about exactly what this means for them, but many of them used terms like "aging gracefully" or some variation of that.

Feeling Good About Appearance/Happiness/Self-acceptance

If we merge these three answers, this theme makes up the largest response group for this question. Some of the answers that fall into this category are especially inspiring.

Staying Physically Active

This was not mentioned as often, but nearly one in ten of the women I spoke to expressly mentioned staying active as their primary definition of optimal aging. Staying physically active also supports general good health, of course. It also supports other aspects of aging well that women mentioned, like "Feeling good about how I look," "Taking care of myself," and slowing down the aging process.

Here are some of my favorite responses to the question, "What would optimal aging look like for you?"

- *For me, a glorious, peaceful, empowering "aging experience" would be to exist in a world where aging and "beauty" aren't attached to a value judgment, where women are free to feel wonderful about themselves and to be wonderful in others' eyes JUST FOR BEING OURSELVES, free from the bondage of our human worth being dependent on what we look like and how we age. How incredible would it be to have the time, energy, money, mental health, etc. that we sacrifice for our looks in this society, to create and build our lives for our highest good... and in turn, the highest good of our communities and society around us?! What a dream, I tell ya. What. A. Dream.*

- *Continuing to be capable of doing things— energy, clear thinking, being active and healthy.*

- *I hope to age gracefully and do the things I can that are affordable to me, nontoxic, and natural... But I also hope to feel little sadness over my appearance and a level of acceptance and appreciation for getting older because it is a gift that not everyone gets. I hope that I can focus more on the beauty within and teach my daughter to do the same.*

- *Having a community of positive women around me cheering me on. Ones that aren't afraid of aging. It's inevitable, let's face it, it's gonna happen anyway! A little work here and there is nice, but I don't want to look like an "alien" and I'd like to do more and more volunteer work as I age.*

- *Being content with my looks.*

- *I'm fit and healthy, still able to do the activities that I enjoy, not having wrinkles in between my eyes, and no gray hair! Yes, I realize I can fix all of these with effort as well as money.*

- *Gradual. With finances that allowed for semi-regular treatments. A focus on lifestyle as a preventative.*

- *Not worrying about looks.*

- *Maintaining fitness, a positive attitude about life, and an attractive and healthy appearance.*

- *Aging gracefully without self-criticism and concern over what other people think.*

- *Aging gracefully, strength training, stress-reducing lifestyle, not living check to check, staying mentally sharp, sleeping well, eating well, more sex drive...*

Inspiring, right? Now it's your turn. What would an optimal aging experience be like for you? _____

_____

_____

_____

_____

WHAT WILL YOU NEED TO
ACHIEVE OPTIMAL AGING?

Goals are good, but having a plan to achieve them is critical. So right after I asked women what optimal aging would look like for them, I asked them what they would need to know, have, do, or be to achieve their version of optimal aging.

What did they say? Money, cosmetic treatments, and information were mentioned more than anything else. Good nutrition, a trusted advisor of some sort, skin care (typically at home or from products rather than cosmetic treatments), and staying active were also frequently mentioned.

Regrettably, less than one in twenty women felt that they were already experiencing optimal aging.

Now let's focus on you. Have you considered what you would need for your vision of optimal aging? If you're curious, use the following questions to explore this idea further. Answer each one with the first thought that comes to mind. There are no right or wrong answers. This is your plan, not based on what you *think* is possible but on what you would achieve if you had no limits.

What would I need to know, do, have, or be to achieve my vision of optimal aging? _____

_____

_____

_____

_____

To achieve my vision of optimal aging, I would benefit from understanding more about _____

_____

_____

_____

_____

The actions I need to take to realize my ideal aging process are _____

_____

_____

_____

_____

_____

In order to age optimally, I would need to have access

to _____

_____

_____

_____

_____

_____

Achieving optimal aging would require me to be someone

who _____

_____

_____

_____

_____

HOW TO CHOOSE A
LONGEVITY PROVIDER

If we want positive results from our approach to aging, we should seek out professionals who can guide us. These experts can jumpstart our progress and make sure we help rather than hurt ourselves. They can also provide motivation when we encounter bumps in the road, with weight loss progress or getting our hormone levels just right for optimal well-being, for example.

Longevity providers are those professionals for all the aspects of your aging. There are many aspects of aging, so there are many types of providers. You probably won't need every kind of longevity provider available, but you should consider working with at least one or two that specialize in an aspect of aging that is especially important to you.

So, what exactly is a longevity provider? A longevity provider is a healthcare provider or other professional committed to working *with* you throughout your aging process who focuses on extending the years of your life spent in good health. Longevity providers typically adopt a holistic approach that combines conventional medicine with preventive care, nutrition, personalized treatment plans, and lifestyle interventions. Their goal is to prevent age-related diseases, support optimal aging, and enhance your quality of life through proactive measures like hormone optimization, advanced diagnostics, personalized supplements, and cutting-edge therapies that address cellular aging and overall well-being. A longevity provider's approach goes beyond treating symptoms; they focus on the root causes of health issues and strategies to slow down or minimize the effects of aging.

When choosing a longevity provider, you may want to consider specialists from both conventional and alternative medicine backgrounds. The following specialists are commonly involved in longevity-focused care. This is a general list and is not meant to be inclusive of all specialties.

Cardiologists manage cardiovascular health and focus on preventing heart disease, hypertension, and stroke.

Chiropractors focus on spinal health and the nervous system to improve mobility, reduce pain, and promote long-term musculoskeletal health.

Dermatologists specialize in skin health and manage age-related skin changes, and sometimes offer cosmetic treatments like laser therapy and injectables.

Endocrinologists manage hormonal imbalances that can affect aging, such as thyroid disorders, diabetes, and menopause or andropause (low testosterone in men).

Exercise Physiologists and Personal Trainers design exercise and fitness programs to improve strength, flexibility, and cardiovascular health as part of a longevity plan.

Functional Medicine Practitioners address the root cause of disease with a holistic approach and emphasize personalized care, lifestyle interventions, and prevention of age-related health issues.

Geneticists and Genomic Medicine Specialists use genetic testing to provide personalized insights into disease risk, aging, and longevity, and focus on personalized prevention plans based on genetic predispositions.

Geriatricians specialize in the health care of older adults and focus on age-related conditions like frailty, cognitive decline, and chronic disease management.

Integrative Medicine Specialists combine traditional medical practices with complementary therapies like acupuncture, herbal medicine, and stress management to focus on overall well-being and long-term health.

Naturopathic Doctors use natural and homeopathic therapies like herbal medicine and nutrition to focus on disease prevention, detoxification, and overall vitality.

Neurologists specialize in brain health and managing cognitive decline, migraines, Alzheimer's, and other neurodegenerative diseases to promote long-term cognitive vitality.

Nutritionists and Dietitians provide guidance on diet and nutrition and create personalized diet plans to promote healthy aging, weight management, and disease prevention.

Psychologists and Therapists who specialize in aging help individuals manage the emotional and psychological aspects of aging such as anxiety, depression, and life transitions, with a focus on mental health, emotional resilience, and cognitive wellness.

Preventive Medicine Physicians focus on preventing disease and maintaining health through screenings, lifestyle counseling, and early interventions.

Regenerative Medicine Specialists focus on therapies to slow the aging process, like hormone replacement therapy, stem cell therapy, and other regenerative techniques that enhance vitality and longevity.

Sleep Medicine Specialists address sleep disorders that can negatively affect longevity, such as sleep apnea and insomnia.

Somatic Therapists focus on the mind-body connection to release stored stress and reduce chronic tension that impacts overall health.

There are many factors to consider when it comes to choosing longevity providers. You are, after all, developing a partnership with a team of providers. You are inviting each one to be part of your journey. You need their expertise, advice, guidance, recommendations, and support. But before you start down this path, you must know where you are going. You will benefit from having answered the questions earlier in this chapter so that you know what you really want for your care. You will also benefit from having confidence in your ability to advocate for yourself. Patience, awareness of your body, and a desire to learn as you go along this path will also help.

282 | THOUGHTFUL AGING

Confidence in working with medical providers is not often talked about, but it can significantly affect your care. Do you find yourself relying on other people to make decisions for you? Do you find yourself asking, "What do you think I should do?" and then unthinkingly following their advice? Automatically following advice is the externalization of authority. If you tend to do this, somewhere in your past, you probably learned that you couldn't trust your own judgment. But you can trust yourself. Only you truly know your needs. It's time to reclaim your authority and be your own advocate. Seeking advice to make informed decisions is a position of confidence, not weakness. When it comes to healthcare, this means you will no longer just take what you get, settle for unanswered questions, or ignore your intuition.

So, how do you know if your doctor is going to work *with* you and support your Thoughtful Aging plan? Much can be revealed by how they interact with you. The examples below show the difference between dismissive and supportive providers and how doctors' comments are often interpreted and relayed to me by patients. While doctors may not use this exact language, their messages to patients are clear. We may not always remember what someone said to us, but we always remember how they made us feel.

Attention

Doctors can be susceptible to an overconfidence that is easy to interpret as dismissiveness or even arrogance.

Here are some examples of what less respectful providers sound like versus respectful providers.

Dismissive of Patient Concerns	Supportive of Patient Concerns
"You're just getting older; there's not much we can do about it."	"I understand your concerns, and while aging brings changes, there are ways we can manage and improve your quality of life."
"It's all in your head."	"Your symptoms are important, and we'll work together to find the cause and appropriate treatment."
"That's just a part of aging; you have to live with it."	"Aging does bring challenges, but let's explore all the options available to make this transition as smooth as possible."

Why these dismissive statements are red flags: They suggest a lack of empathy and a willingness to dismiss legitimate concerns without exploring potential solutions or offering support.

Attitude

Some doctors believe that they know what is best for their patients regardless of their patients' input. This leaves patients feeling alienated. Here are some examples of what this attitude can sound like.

Rigid or Paternalistic Attitude	Values Your Intuition
"I'm the doctor, and I know what's best for you."	"Your input is valuable, and together we can decide what's best for your health."
"There's no need for you to look up information online; just trust me."	"It's great that you're researching your condition; let's discuss what you've learned and how it applies to your care."
"I don't think you need a second opinion."	"I always support getting a second opinion if it helps you feel more confident in your care decisions."

Why a rigid or paternalistic attitude is a red flag: A collaborative physician should value your input and encourage you to be informed and involved in your own care. A paternalistic attitude can indicate a reluctance to engage in shared decision-making.

Alternative Therapies

Some doctors dismiss alternative or integrative therapies because they believe these therapies are unproven or unnecessary. This can leave the patient feeling invalidated. Here's a comparison of how doctors who embrace or resist alternative therapies may approach these conversations.

Unwilling to Consider Alternative or Integrative Therapies	Considers Alternative or Integrative Therapies
"I don't believe in alternative medicine; it's not worth discussing."	"Let's discuss any natural or alternative treatments you're interested in and see how they might complement your care."
"You should stop taking any supplements or herbal remedies immediately."	"If you're taking any supplements or herbal remedies, let's review them together to ensure they fit into your treatment plan."

"There's no evidence for those natural treatments, so don't waste your time."	"While there may not yet be extensive research on some natural treatments, I'm open to exploring options that align with your values."

Why unwillingness to consider alternative or integrative therapies is a red flag: A collaborative physician should be open to discussing and integrating alternative therapies into your care plan if they align with your health goals. Dismissing these options outright may indicate a lack of respect for your preferences.

Preventive Care

Doctors who primarily focus on treating existing conditions often overlook preventive care. This makes it difficult for patients to take charge of their health. Here's how a lack of focus on preventive care compares to a proactive approach.

Lack of Focus on Preventive Care	Emphasis on Preventive Care
"We'll address problems as they arise; no need to worry about prevention right now."	"Prevention is key to healthy aging; let's work on strategies to keep you feeling your best."
"Just come back when something is really wrong."	"I'm here to help you stay healthy, not just treat issues when they arise. Regular checkups are a big part of that."
"You're fine for now, so there's no point in doing more tests or making lifestyle changes."	"Even if you're feeling well, there are steps we can take now to prevent future health issues."

Why a lack of focus on preventive care is a red flag: A proactive physician should emphasize preventive care and work with you to reduce the risk of future health problems. A lack of interest in prevention may indicate a reactive rather than a proactive approach.

Personalized Care

Doctors often follow strict protocols without considering individual patient circumstances. This diminishes patient autonomy and can leave them feeling unheard. Here's how inflexible and flexible doctors handle treatment plans.

Inflexibility with Treatment Plans	Flexibility with Treatment Plans
"This is the only treatment option available to you."	"There are several treatment options available; let's review them and find what works best for you."
"You have to follow this treatment exactly as I prescribe it, no exceptions."	"I'm here to tailor your treatment to fit your life and preferences. Let's find a plan that suits you."
"I don't adjust treatment plans based on patient preferences."	"I'm open to adjusting your treatment plan based on your experiences and feedback."

Why inflexibility in treatment plans is a red flag: A collaborative physician should be willing to discuss different treatment options and tailor a plan that fits your individual needs and preferences.

Communication

Some doctors' communication skills are better than others. Poor communication skills can cause feelings of isolation and misunderstanding for the patient and hinder effective care. Here are some examples of minimal versus effective communication.

Minimal Communication or Engagement	Enhancing Communication and Engagement
"We don't need to spend too much time discussing your questions."	"I'm here to answer any questions you have; your understanding is important to me."
"I don't have time to explain everything; just follow the instructions."	"Let's take the time to go over your treatment plan in detail so you feel confident moving forward."

"There's no need for a follow-up unless something goes wrong."	"I'd like to schedule regular follow-ups to make sure everything is on track and address any concerns."

Why minimal communication or engagement is a red flag: Effective communication and patient engagement are crucial for a collaborative relationship. If a physician seems uninterested in answering your questions or keeping you informed, it could be a sign that they are not committed to working with you as a partner in your health.

Medications

Doctors with a narrow view of patient care typically overemphasize medications or procedures without adequately considering lifestyle factors. This leaves patients feeling reliant on treatments rather than inspired to make lifestyle changes. Here are examples of overemphasis on medications compared to a balanced approach.

Overemphasis on Medication or Procedures Without Considering Lifestyle	A Balanced Approach to Medications and Procedures
"Medication is the only way to manage this condition."	"Medication is one option, but let's also discuss lifestyle changes and other therapies that could help."
"There's no point in making lifestyle changes; just take the pill."	"Lifestyle adjustments can be powerful; let's explore what changes might benefit you most."
"Surgery is the best option, and other treatments are not worth considering."	"Surgery is one possibility, but I'm here to discuss all the options with you before making a decision."

Why overemphasis on medication or procedures is a red flag: A proactive, holistic approach should consider lifestyle changes, diet, exercise, and other noninvasive options before resorting to medication or surgery as the first line of treatment.

Patient Autonomy

Doctors who disregard patient autonomy make decisions without fully considering the patient's preferences or values, leading to feelings of mistrust and undermining the patient's confidence in their ability to take an active role in their health care. Here's a comparison of what it sounds like when a doctor disregards patient autonomy versus when they respect it.

Disregard for Patient Autonomy	Respect for Patient Autonomy
"I don't think you need to be involved in every decision."	"You should be involved in every decision about your health; your perspective is crucial."
"You should just trust me without questioning the treatment plan."	"Your trust is important, and I'm here to explain every step of your treatment plan."
"Your preferences don't matter as much as what I think is best."	"Your preferences guide our decisions, and I'm here to support what's best for you."

Why disregard for patient autonomy is a red flag: Respect for patient autonomy is fundamental to a collaborative relationship. If a physician downplays your role in decision-making, it may indicate a lack of respect for your rights and preferences.

Collaborative Care

Doctors can sometimes hold a negative attitude toward collaborative care, viewing it as a challenge to their authority or expertise.

Negative Attitude Toward Collaborative Care	Supportive of Collaborative Care
"You don't need to see any other specialists; I can handle everything."	"If you need to see a specialist or another healthcare provider, I'm happy to coordinate your care."
"I don't collaborate with other types of healthcare providers like naturopaths or therapists."	"I'm open to collaborating with other providers, including naturopaths and therapists, to ensure comprehensive care."

"There's no point in integrating care from different disciplines."	"Integrating care from different disciplines can be very beneficial; let's consider all the options together."

Why a negative attitude toward collaborative care is a red flag: A physician should be open to working with other healthcare providers to ensure comprehensive care. A negative attitude toward collaboration may indicate a disingenuous approach to your health.

SIX STEPS TO CHOOSING A LONGEVITY PROVIDER

Advocating for your needs as you create a Thoughtful Aging plan may feel new to you. Choosing a longevity provider requires an understanding of your health goals, lifestyle, and how that provider's expertise can support your journey. Here is a six-step approach to the process of choosing a longevity provider.

1. Research Providers: Start by researching providers who specialize in any of the areas listed earlier in this chapter. There are also many nurse practitioners and physician assistants who provide excellent care and would be great assets in your Thoughtful Aging journey. You might also consider acupuncturists and massage therapists for treatment support. Look for those with reputable credentials and a strong background in preventive care, wellness, and age management.

2. Check Experience and Specialization: Don't get hung up on credentials, but do be sure the provider has experience in the areas that matter most to you, such as hormone optimization, nutrition, genetic testing, or advanced diagnostic techniques. Reviews and testimonials can provide insight into a provider's bedside manner and their ability to engage in conversation.

3. Schedule an Initial Consultation: Schedule a consultation to discuss your goals, concerns, and expectations. This meeting will give you a sense of the provider's communication style and whether you feel comfortable with them. Come prepared with questions. When scheduling initial appointments, push for a longer appointment time. The minimum length of any initial appointment with a new provider should be thirty minutes. You can ask for forty-five or even up to sixty minutes when scheduling. They may tell you it's not possible, but gently persist. They may need to get approval from management to schedule that much time, but it can be done.

4. Ask Key Questions: What is your approach to longevity care, and how do you tailor it to individual needs?

What specific tests and assessments do you use to evaluate a person's biological age and overall health?

How do you integrate lifestyle factors such as diet, exercise, sleep, and stress management into your treatment plans?

What kind of ongoing support or follow-up care do you offer to monitor progress and adjust treatments?

Can you provide examples of successful outcomes or case studies similar to my situation?

How do you stay updated on the latest advancements in longevity and aging research?

Can you recommend supplements specific to my brain and body health and aging needs?

Are you open to collaborating with other multidisciplinary providers such as acupuncturists, chiropractors, mental health therapists, massage therapists, naturopathic doctors, etc.? (Hint: If their response is no, find another provider.)

5. Evaluate Compatibility: Consider whether the provider's philosophy aligns with your personal health values and whether they offer a comprehensive, individualized plan rather than a one-size-fits-all approach.

6. Review Costs and Commitment: Understand the financial commitment involved, including the cost of initial consultations, ongoing treatments, and any recommended supplements or therapies. If you have insurance, check your benefits. In most cases, medical offices do this at the time of scheduling. However, if you are going to take charge of your health, it is your responsibility to know your benefits and co-pays.

COMMUNICATING WITH
YOUR PROVIDER

If you find that you are getting pushback from your provider as you communicate your desires and needs, use the following responses to keep dialogue open:

Request a Second Opinion: Politely express your intention to seek a second opinion. This can prompt your provider to reconsider their stance or at least talk to you more like an equal partner in your care. Seeking second opinions can also be highly educational for you. Options are always a good thing.

Ask for Clarification: Patients often ask for a detailed explanation of their provider's reasoning. You could ask questions like, "Can you explain why you believe this is the best course of action?" or "What are the risks or drawbacks of considering other treatments?"

Present Research or Information: If you've researched alternative treatments, share credible sources or studies with your provider. Phrasing it as "I've read about [alternative treatment]—could we discuss if that might be appropriate in my case?" can show that you're informed and engaged.

Express Concerns About Current Treatment: Sometimes, patients voice their concerns by saying, "I'm not comfortable with the current approach and would like to explore other options." This can open the door to a more collaborative discussion.

Request a Referral: If the provider remains resistant, you might ask for a referral to a specialist or a healthcare provider who is more open to discussing a broader range of options.

Advocate for Shared Decision-Making: Remind the provider of the importance of shared decision-making in your care, saying something like, "I value your expertise, but I'd like us to work together to find a treatment plan that aligns with my goals and concerns."

Consider a Change in Providers: If the provider consistently dismisses your concerns or preferences, it may be necessary to consider finding a new provider who is more aligned with your healthcare philosophy.

The goal of these conversations is to establish a more open and collaborative relationship between you and your provider. If you are not experiencing a collaborative connection with your provider, that's okay. Respect their position and don't take it personally. Consider seeking a provider who is willing to collaborate with you so that your healthcare needs and preferences are respected.

We live in a world of opportunities. With the help of science, our options for how we age, how well we age, and what effects we allow aging to have on our day-to-day lives have expanded greatly. Taking the time to find the right longevity provider will help ensure you are making informed decisions that support your health and longevity goals.

IT'S NOT TOO LATE

If you're feeling like it's too late to begin this journey, I can assure you, it is not. As we contemplate major changes, the process may seem overwhelming. But small steps are all that is required. One decision to choose gratitude, one genuine compliment to brighten another woman's day, one courageous step toward self-care is all that it takes.

Let curiosity be your guide. See what works for you. See what habits you *can* build, no matter how small they might seem. Explore resources within your budget. Be vulnerable with your friends—ask how they manage aging and self-care as a way to learn, not judge. Educate yourself so you can be proactive about your health.

The world needs you: bold, authentic, beautiful you. Keep moving forward with the unwavering belief that you deserve all the love, joy, and fulfillment life has to offer.

Afterword

As we come to the close of this book, I am reminded of the profound difference between merely looking at someone versus truly seeing them. For as long as I can remember, this distinction has shaped my understanding of the need for our human souls to be connected to the beauty of the world around us. It is central to the message of Thoughtful Aging. It is an invitation to embrace not just the surface, but the deep beauty that rests in the essence of who we are as we grow older.

My spiritual upbringing taught me that we are all equal, created by design, each with a purpose that is uniquely ours. This sense of sacred intention has guided me, affirming that we are more than our physical bodies, our achievements, or our roles. We are vessels of a deeper love that transcends the limitations of time, offering us the opportunity to touch others with the wisdom and grace that come with age.

There is a universal love that calls to each of us—a gentle, quiet, consistent whisper to our hearts. It is a love that I have both witnessed and experienced, and it is this love that reminds us of our worth, our beauty, and our purpose. It invites us to return to ourselves, to shed the layers of doubt and insecurity that others placed upon us so that we may stand in truth and reflect the beauty that we carry within.

This journey of restoring honor to aging is not just for our own healing, but also for the healing of those around us. By reclaiming our value and embracing the unique gifts that aging offers us, we create space for others to do the same. When we see ourselves clearly, we help others see themselves in the same compassionate light.

I hope that as you turn these last pages, you feel equipped to step forward with renewed confidence in your own journey. May you be inspired to honor the signs of life written on your skin, in your heart, and in your soul, knowing that in doing so, you are paving the way for others to recognize their own beauty, purpose, and worth. The path of Thoughtful Aging is a shared one, and together, we restore honor to the process, one graceful step at a time.

Thank you for walking this path with me. May you continue to see and be seen with love and honor, knowing *you are beautiful, just as you are.*

—A.W.

Get a free, personalized Thoughtful Aging Plan

Want a more detailed plan for your care?
Go to ThoughtfulAgingAssessment.com
to get a free, personalized plan
delivered to your inbox.

Notes

Chapter 1

1   Renee Engeln, PhD, *Beauty Sick: How the Cultural Obsession with Appearance Hurts Girls and Women* (New York, NY: HarperCollins Publishers, 2017).

2   Kim Parker, Juliana Horowitz and Renee Stepler, "On Gender Differences, No Consensus on Nature vs. Nurture," Pew Research Center, December 5, 2017, https://www.pewresearch.org/wp-content/ uploads/sites/20/2017/12/Gender-report-December-2017-FINAL.pdf, accessed October 11, 2024.

3   Colette Thayer, Stephanie Childs, Angela Houghton, and Alicia R. Williams, "Keeping Beauty Real: Media's Missed Opportunity? Mirror/Mirror: AARP 2023 Survey of Women's Reflections on Beauty, Age, and Media," AARP, September 2023, https://doi.org/10.26419/ res.00703.001, accessed October 11, 2024.

4   AARP Research, "Mirror/Mirror," September 2023

5   AARP Research, "Mirror/Mirror," September 2023

6 Jocelyn Gecker, "Young girls are using anti-aging products they see on social media. The harm is more than skin deep," Associated Press, August 31, 2024, https://apnews.com/article/influenced-skincare-routine-mental-health-f59bb091 14ab93323e3a47197a1ad914, accessed October 11, 2024.

7 The Benchmarking Company, "She's (Anti-) Aging Beautifully—Infographic Series: #3," April 10, 2023, https://benchmarkingcompany.com/news-archive/shes-anti-aging-beautifully-infographic-series-3/, accessed October 11, 2024.

8 StyleSeat, "People in These U.S. States Are Rewriting the Rules on Aging, Study Finds," October 5, 2023, https://www.styleseat.com/blog/states-rewriting-rules-on-aging/, accessed October 11, 2024.

9 Engeln, *Beauty Sick*

10 AARP Research, "Mirror/Mirror," September 2023

11 World Happiness Report, "World Happiness Report 2024," https://worldhappiness.report, accessed October 11, 2024.

12 AARP Research, "Mirror/Mirror: AARP Survey of Women's Reflections on Beauty, Age, and Media™," AARP, May 2021, https://www.aarp.org/content/dam/aarp/research/surveys_statistics/life-leisure/2021/mirror-mirror-women-beauty-media.doi.10.26419-2Fres.00429.001.pdf, accessed October 11, 2024.

13 Alicia R. Williams, "What Is Beauty? Older Adults Have a Better Grasp Than the Still-Improving Beauty Industry," AARP, March 12, 2024, https://www.aarp.org/pri/

topics/aging-experience/demographics/mirror-mirror-five-year-retrospective.html, accessed October 11, 2024.

Chapter 2

14 Peter Leithart, "Called to Beauty," Theopolis, April 9, 2013, https://theopolisinstitute.com/leithart_post/called-to-beauty/, accessed October 11, 2024.

15 Carol Dweck, *Mindset: The New Psychology of Success* (New York, NY: Random House, 2006).

Chapter 3

16 Dr. Gabor Maté, *The Myth of Normal: Trauma, Illness, and Healing in a Toxic Culture* (New York, NY: Avery Publishing, 2022).

17 This Bruce Lee "quote" is not actually a quote. It is basically a summary of his philosophy that has been widely used and is attributed to him.

Chapter 5

18 *Bridgetown Audio Podcast*, Episode 602, "Daily: You Are A Body," March 8, 2021, https://podcasts.apple.com/us/podcast/daily-you-are-a-body/id84246334?i=1000512179546, accessed October 11, 2024. Tristen approved an edited transcription of part of her segment and gave her permission for me to use it here.

19 AARP Research, "Mirror/Mirror: AARP Survey Of Women's Reflections On Beauty, Age, And Media™—A Five-Year Retrospective," AARP, January 2024, https://www.aarp.org/content/dam/aarp/research/topics/aging-experience/demographics/mirror-mirror-five-year-retrospective.doi.10.26419-2fres.00758.001.pdf, accessed October 11, 2024.

20 AARP Research, "Mirror/Mirror," January 2024

21 Definition of "vanity." Merriam-Webster, https://www.merriam-webster.com/dictionary/vanity, accessed October 11, 2024.

Chapter 6

22 S. E. Taylor, L. C. Klein, B. P. Lewis, T. L. Gruenewald, R. A. Gurung, and J. A. Updegraff, "Biobehavioral responses to stress in females: Tend-and-befriend, not fight-or-flight," *Psychological Review,* 107(3), 2000, https://taylorlab.psych.ucla.edu/wp-content/uploads/sites/5/2014/11/2011_Tend-and-Befriend-Theory.pdf, accessed October 11, 2024.

23 Marco Iacoboni, *Mirroring People: The New Science of How We Connect* (New York, NY: Farrar, Straus and Giroux, 2008).

24 Paraphrased from Dr. Curt Thompson, *The Soul of Desire: Discovering the Neuroscience of Longing, Beauty, and Community* (Lisle, IL: InterVarsity Press, 2021).

25 Dr. Christie Hartman, PhD, "Loneliness Statistics: By Country, Demographics & More," The Roots of Loneliness Project, updated March 27, 2024,

https://www.rootsofloneliness.com/loneliness-statistics, accessed October 11, 2024.

26 BBC, "Dunbar's number: Why we can only maintain 150 relationships," October 9, 2019, https://www.bbc.com/future/article/20191001-dunbars-number-why-we-can-only-maintain-150-relationships, accessed October 11, 2024.

Also see Selby Frame, "Julianne Holt-Lunstad probes loneliness, social connections," American Psychological Association, 2017, https://www.apa.org/members/content/holt-lunstad-loneliness-social-connections, accessed October 11, 2024.

27 David Brooks, *How to Know a Person: The Art of Seeing Others Deeply and Being Deeply Seen* (New York, NY: Random House, 2023).

28 Melody Beattie, *Codependent No More: How to Stop Controlling Others and Start Caring for Yourself* (Center City, MN: Hazelden Publishing, 1986).

29 Diane Ulicsni website, https://www.dianeu.com/home/, accessed 24 October, 2024.

Chapter 7

30 This quote is often attributed to David Bowie.

Chapter 8

31 Taylor W. Schmitz, Eve De Rosa and Adam K. Anderson, "Opposing Influences of Affective State Valence on Visual Cortical Encoding," *The Journal of Neuroscience,* Vol. 29, Issue

22, June 2009, 29 (22) 7199-7207, https://doi.org/10.1523/JNEUROSCI.5387-08.2009, accessed October 11, 2024.

32 Jim Sollisch, "The Cure for Decision Fatigue," *Wall Street Journal,* June 10, 2016, https://wsj.com/articles/the-cure-for-decision-fatigue-1465596928, accessed October 11, 2024.

33 Christine Comaford, "Got Inner Peace? 5 Ways To Get It NOW," Forbes, updated November 7, 2013, https://www.forbes.com/sites/christinecomaford/2012/04/04/got-inner-peace-5-ways-to-get-it-now/, accessed October 11, 2024.

Chapter 9

34 *On Being with Krista Tippett* podcast, Episode 1032, "John O'Donohue—The Inner Landscape of Beauty," February 10, 2022, https://podcasts.apple.com/us/podcast/on-being-with-krista-tippett/id150892556?i=1000550716562, accessed October 11, 2024.

35 AARP Research, "Mirror/Mirror," January 2024

36 C.S. Lewis, *The Weight of Glory and Other Addresses* (New York, NY: The MacMillan Company, 1949).

Chapter 10

37 UCLA Health, "Should you take collagen supplements?" September 30, 2022, https://www.uclahealth.org/news/article/should-you-take-collagen-supplement, accessed October 11, 2024.

38 John Hopkins Medicine, "Introduction to Menopause," 2024, https://www.hopkinsmedicine.org/health/conditions-and-diseases/introduction-to-menopause, accessed October 11, 2024.

39 University Hospitals "The Science of Health" blog, "The Connection Between Menopause & Belly Fat," August 24, 2023, https://www.uhhospitals.org/blog/articles/2023/08/the-connection-between-menopause-and-belly-fat, accessed October 11, 2024.

Acknowledgments

GB—your quiet strength and thoughtful reflections have guided me, helping me to see both my strengths and my shadows, always reminding me to stay rooted in truth. This work would not have been possible without your loving encouragement and the depth of your heart. Thank you for your unwavering love, support, and insights as I found my way back to myself.

Pam Neely at Authority Books Publishing. An author is only as good as her editor. I am confident that our paths crossed through divine intervention. I admire your professionalism, patience, strategic planning, and ninja-like skills in navigating my curveballs. I want to be you when I grow up.

To the Bridgeport patients who have entrusted us with their care—it has been a profound privilege to be part of your lives, to witness your strength, resilience, and courage in moments of vulnerability. It is with immense gratitude that I acknowledge the role you've played in my journey. Your stories have not only enriched this work but have also reminded me of the sacredness of the human connection we are privileged to share.

And to the Bridgeport employees, past and present—thank you for the invaluable role you have played in my journey. Through the many transitions and challenges life has presented, you have been there—supporting not only the business but also my personal growth as a leader and as a human being. I am eternally grateful for the trust you have placed in me, for the community we've built together, and for the lessons we've learned from one another. You have my deepest gratitude and respect.

Mark Groves—thank you for inspiring me to see beyond the surface, to understand that growth comes not from conformity but from the willingness to explore the unknown. Your example of authenticity, strength, and vulnerability has deeply shaped my journey, and this work is a reflection of the lessons you have shared.

About Alina Wilson

Alina Wilson is a mother and grandmother, entrepreneur, philanthropist, and advocate for women's well-being. Her life's work is shaped by one goal: to help women discover and embrace their true beauty, both inside and out.

As a mother and grandmother, she has developed a profound understanding of the complexities of womanhood and the importance of self-discovery and self-acceptance.

As the founder of Bridgeport Laser & Wellness Center, a successful medical spa established in 2007, she has mentored and supported numerous women in their personal and professional growth. Her leadership is heart-centered, grounded in a spiritual foundation, and dedicated to inspiring compassion-based connection.

Alina is a dedicated philanthropist. She serves on the board of directors for the Portland-based organization Gather:Make:Shelter. She is also a writer who encourages women to embrace their unique beauty and live authentically.

Her commitment to living with purpose and passion reflects the transformative power of embracing one's true beauty. She hopes to continue inspiring women on their own personal journeys.

Contact

Alina Wilson is available for speaking engagements. Reach out to hello@thoughtfulagingbook.com for more information.

If you are interested in ordering copies of Thoughtful Aging in bulk, or would like to discuss creating a customized version of Thoughtful Aging for your organization or an event, send an inquiry to hello@thoughtfulagingbook.com.

Thoughtful Aging is on social media at:

- https://www.instagram.com/thoughtfulagingbook

- https://www.facebook.com/thoughtfulagingbook/

- https://thoughtfulaging.substack.com/

- https://www.youtube.com/@thoughtfulaging

Sign up for the Thoughtful Aging newsletter at ThoughtfulAgingBook.com